Transpersonal Mental Health Care

Theory and Practice

By
Professor Oluwafemi Emmanuel Esan

Transpersonalmentalhealthclinic.com

Table of Contents

Introduction

Transpersonal Mental Healthcare

Transpersonal mental health is a psychology field that combines modern psychology ideas and various religious and cultural traditions to help people achieve well-being, self-awareness, and personal growth. It's sometimes called spiritual psychology because it combines scientific and spiritual concepts.

Transpersonal Mental Health Care is a type of mental health care that doesn't focus on a person's body and mind only but the health of a person's spirit. This type of mental health care emphasizes a person's spiritual path or spiritual enlightenment during his life. Transpersonal Mental Health Care principles are based on the ontological foundation of creationism.

Creationism is the belief that God created the universe, and the various life forms out of nothing (ex nihilo). We believe a healthy spiritual life is the foundation for sound mental health.

The spiritual framework places spirituality as the core of the person. It regards an individual's spirit as one's being, unharmed by injury or illness, rather than as a component. The core principle of Transpersonal Mental Healthcare is built on a spiritual framework. One of the primary limitations of psychology is the difficulty in studying complex human behaviour.

Many factors influence human behaviour, including biology, culture, socialization, and personal experience. This complexity makes it challenging to study human behaviour in a controlled and systematic way. The medical model can have a narrow focus on biological factors, which can lead to a reductionist view of mental illness. It can neglect other important factors, such as social, psychological and spiritual factors.

The medical model can fail to account for the fact that psychotherapy is an interpersonal process, not a medical procedure. It can also fail to account for the fact that most clients use psychotherapy for support and guidance, not treatment.

Another limitation of the medical model is that it tends to pathologize ordinary human experiences and behaviours, such as sadness or anxiety. This can lead to over-diagnosis and over-treatment of mental health issues, which can have negative consequences for individuals who may be unnecessarily labelled as mentally ill.

The spiritual medical model encourages a more holistic understanding of health and the integration of various therapeutic modalities. Embracing a patient's spiritual beliefs can help healthcare providers better understand human nature and be more culturally sensitive.

By respecting a patient's subjective realities, such as their belief in life after death, healthcare providers can improve the effectiveness of mental health initiatives. Spirituality can provide a sense of meaning, which can help people accept and live with problems that might otherwise seem insurmountable. When a person's spirit, body, and mind are aligned, their hormones can be better regulated, which can help their body function.

When you get spiritual health treatment, you may be better able to create a soothing environment around you. While this may not seem like a big deal, your environment plays a role in your mental and physical wellness. Including spiritual care in your overall healthcare can benefit your health.

About the author

Professor Oluwafemi Esan, a Nigerian-born British national, is a distinguished professional with multiple leadership positions in various fields. He is the Vice-Chancellor of African Union University and the State of African Diaspora Roving Ambassador.

A Transpersonal Psychology and Education professor, he is also an ordained Prophet with over 20 years of international prophetic ministry experience. He was born in the city of Ilesha, in Osun state, Nigeria.

He had four years of medical education at the College of Medicine at the University of Ibadan with an MBBS part 1 examination (Anatomy, Physiology, and Biochemistry) before embarking on theological training, leading to his ministerial ordination. An academic missionary Evangelist.

Professor Esan is a Transpersonal Therapist with over a decade of practice experience, specializing in Transpersonal Mental Health interventions. He holds an MSc in Coaching Psychology from the University of East London and a Master of Education (MEd) from Canterbury Christ Church University. A qualified secondary school teacher, an FE college lecturer, and a university lecturer.

He obtained an MA in higher education, a PGCHE from Anglia Ruskin University, and a PGCE level 7 from the University of Greenwich. His expertise in transpersonal psychology, backed by 12 years of research, solidifies his position as a leading authority in the field.

He serves as the Principal Consultant of the Transpersonal Mental Health Clinic and Vice-Chancellor of El-Roi London Academy and University. Additionally, he serves as the Ambassador of the Sovereign Kingdom of Hawaii to the United Kingdom and the European Union.

He founded El-roi London University, an Indigenous curriculum-based higher education provider. His passion is to provide a platform for the decolonization of the African Curriculum and liberation from the neo-colonization of the intellectual life of the African people.

In collaboration with El-Roi London University, he was conferred a doctorate in Transpersonal Coaching Psychology by the Kingdom of Hawaii Royal Accreditation Commission (KOHRAC). Professor Esan utilizes his skills to facilitate healing and self-discovery as a certified Transpersonal Mental Health Therapist and Consultant in Transpersonal Psychology.

As Vice-Chancellor and Global Academic Director, Professor Esan has played a pivotal role in shaping academic excellence and innovation at El-Roi London Academy and University. He has trained over 1000 trainee teachers in the UK in teacher training and development, leaving an indelible mark on the educational landscape.

Chapter 1- Transpersonal Psychology in Mental Health

Transpersonal psychology, also known as spiritual psychology, is a branch of psychology that studies the spiritual and metaphysical aspects of human experience. It aims to understand the more profound meaning and purpose of human experiences and the connection between the self and a higher consciousness.

Transpersonal psychology incorporates ideas from various religious and cultural traditions and modern psychological theories, philosophy, literature, **health theories,** art, social theory, and cognition science. (Hartelius, Caplan, and Rardin, 2007).

Transpersonal psychology investigates **spiritual practices** and experiences and their relationship to psychological models and concepts. It can help people reach their fullest potential and transcend the limitations of their ego. For example, a 2022 study found that transpersonal therapy was effective in reducing symptoms of depression in breast cancer patients. (Grof, 2008).

Transpersonal psychology is based partly on Abraham Maslow's research on self-actualization and his belief that creativity, experiences, personal actions, and altruism exist outside the ordinary personality. Transpersonal psychology is a branch of psychology focused on studying the spiritual and transcendental aspects of the human experience.

It is an approach that seeks to understand how the connection between the self and our higher consciousness can lead to growth and self-development. Transpersonal is an adjective that means extending beyond the personal or individual. It can also refer to psychology or psychotherapy focusing on esoteric mental experiences, such as mysticism and altered states of consciousness. (Lajoie, and Shapiro, 1992)

The transpersonal has been defined as experiences in which the sense of identity or self extends beyond (trans) the individual or personal to encompass broader aspects of humankind, life, psyche, or cosmos—extending or going beyond the personal or individual and relating to, or being psychology or psychotherapy concerned especially with esoteric mental experience (such as mysticism and altered states of consciousness) beyond the usual limits of ego and personality.

The transpersonal self is not identified exclusively with the separate self but has discovered the universal ground of being that sustains it by virtue of direct experience and disidentification from ego. (Lajoie, and Shapiro, 1992)

Your Spiritual Self is you in your most beautiful and powerful form. It is the authentic self, the unconditioned part, the you without patterns. This is personal for each of us, so there is no need to get caught up in the language. The source of inner wisdom and resilience that is untouched by patterns.

Accessing the spiritual self can lead to feelings of happiness, peace, and centring, and actions can align with purpose. Others say that spiritual people have positive attitudes and characteristics, such as being humble, calm, and centred, and positively relating to others. Some ways to connect with the spiritual self include Reconnecting with an inner guide and intuition and Practicing spiritual self-care. (Ausar, Lekhak, and Candela, 2021)

Spiritual self-care can involve activities that help you connect with a **higher power,** express gratitude, or achieve balance and well-being. It can help people connect with a higher power, seek guidance, or express gratitude.

Spiritual self-care includes reading and **reflecting on scripture,** listening to inspirational music, attending virtual spiritual activities, Acting in kindness, and working towards non-materialistic goals. Spiritual self-care involves engaging in activities that turn our attention inward and reconnect us with ourselves. Spiritual self-care helps us more profoundly clarify what matters most to us and what we believe in. (Ausar, Lekhak, and Candela, 2021)

Spiritual health is a broad term that refers to a person's connection to something greater than themselves, such as a higher power, energy, or inner peace. It can also include a person's values, beliefs, and morals, giving them a sense of purpose and meaning in life.

Spiritually healthy people may feel at peace with life, even during difficult times, and have a strong sense of connection to a community or calling. Spiritual health is achieved when you feel at peace with life. It is when you can find hope and comfort in even the most challenging times.

Ultimately, it can help support you as you experience life. Spirituality is different for everyone. Spiritual wellness is having a set of principles, values, beliefs, and morals that give you a sense of meaning and purpose in your life. This, and being connected to something greater than yourself, will guide your actions through life. (Bensley, 1991).

Spirituality involves exploring specific universal themes – love, compassion, altruism, life after death, wisdom, and truth, with the knowledge that some people, such as saints or enlightened individuals, have achieved and manifested higher levels of development than the ordinary person.

Spiritual purpose is a person's search for meaning and purpose in life, often in a context separate from organized religion. It can also involve personal growth or transformation, including seeking out religious experiences, believing in a supernatural realm or afterlife, or making sense of one's inner dimension.

Spiritual well-being is the ability to establish meaning and find purpose through the fusion of art, nature, and a sense of connection beyond the self. It can benefit our overall well-being by cultivating both our sense of inner understanding and our sense of place.

Being spiritual can relieve you from dependence on material things and help you to understand your life's greater purpose. Spirituality can also be used to cope with change or uncertainty. If you want to learn about your God-given purpose, reading your Bible is a great place to start. Praying for direction: Prayer is another excellent way to discover and fulfil our God-given purpose. Biblical Psychology tells us to ask God for what we need, so when you need direction, ask God for it in prayer. (Bensley, 1991).

Your life purpose consists of the central motivating aims of your life—the reasons you get up in the morning. Purpose can guide life decisions, influence behaviour, shape goals, offer a sense of direction, and create meaning. For some people, purpose is connected to vocation—meaningful, satisfying work. Determining your passions often helps you figure out what God has called you to do.

It's usually said that God works at the intersection of **our gifts and our passions.** Where do your gifts meet your passions? That may be God's purpose for you. You can define your definite purpose by identifying your specific goal in life and visualizing a future where you have fulfilled your desires. Create a specific plan to achieve your goals and start on it right away. (Hawks, 1994)

The Impact of Spirituality on Mental Health encourages people to have better relationships with themselves, others, and the unknown. Spirituality can help you deal with stress by giving you a sense of peace, purpose, and forgiveness. It often becomes more important in times of emotional stress or illness. Spirituality can also play a role in mental health through Coping Mechanisms: In times of adversity, individuals often turn to their spiritual beliefs as a source of comfort and resilience. Practices such as prayer, meditation, and rituals offer a structured way to manage stress and anxiety.

Research on the impact of spirituality on the brain Shows that spiritual experiences shift perception and can moderate the effects of stress on mental health. This study saw decreased activation in the parts of the brain responsible for stress and increased activity in the parts of the brain responsible for connection with others.

Spiritual practices like prayer or meditation can help you quiet the mind and focus on the present so you can let go of the negative chatter that's fueling your anxiety. You'll feel a sense of purpose. Cultivating your spirituality can help you uncover what's most important in your life. (Hawks, 1994)

Spiritual resilience is maintaining one's sense of purpose and self through adversity, stress, and trauma using **internal and external spiritual resources.** It can be an everyday occurrence and can be transformative. Spirituality can be defined as a quest for meaning, purpose, or something larger than ourselves.

It can be secular or non-secular, religious or not about religion at all. Spiritual resilience enables one to Build inner strength, Make meaning of experiences, Behave ethically, Persevere through challenges, and

Be resilient in the face of adversity. Spiritual resilience is the core element of Transpersonal mental health care. (Jaberi, et al, 2019)

Transpersonal Mental Health Care is a type of mental health care that doesn't focus on a person's body and mind only but the health of a person's spirit.

This type of mental health care emphasizes a person's spiritual path or enlightenment during life. Many people are also working toward becoming more spiritually aware. The word "transpersonal" loosely translates to beyond the person or beyond the self. Nearly anyone can benefit from transpersonal mental health care. However, some people may respect this type of mental health therapy more than others.

For instance, people looking to explore their spiritual sides and those open to new experiences will often benefit more from transpersonal mental health care. Transpersonal mental health care takes a holistic approach to treatment with an emphasis on **spirituality.** This mental health care practice addresses the client's mental, physical, social, emotional, creative, and intellectual needs to facilitate healing and growth. (Jaberi, et al, 2019)

Reference

- Hartelius, G., Caplan, M. and Rardin, M.A., 2007. Transpersonal psychology: Defining the past, divining the future. The Humanistic Psychologist, 35(2), pp.135-160.

- Grof, S., 2008. Brief history of transpersonal psychology. International Journal of Transpersonal Studies, 27(1), p.6.
- Lajoie, D.H. and Shapiro, S.I., 1992. Definitions of transpersonal psychology: The first twenty-three years. The Journal of Transpersonal Psychology, 24(1), p.79.
- Ausar, K., Lekhak, N. and Candela, L., 2021. Nurse spiritual self-care: A scoping review. Nursing Outlook, 69(4), pp.660-671.
- Bensley, R.J., 1991. Defining spiritual health: A review of the literature. Journal of Health Education, 22(5), pp.287-290.
- Hawks, S., 1994. Spiritual health: Definition and theory. Wellness perspectives, 10(4).
- Jaberi, A., Momennasab, M., Yektatalab, S., Ebadi, A. and Cheraghi, M.A., 2019. Spiritual health: A concept analysis. Journal of religion and health, 58, pp.1537-1560.

Chapter 2- Transpersonal Ontology Based On Biblical Creationism.

Ontology, at its simplest, is the study of **existence.** But it is much more than that, too. Ontology is also the study of how we determine if things **exist or not,** as well as the classification of existence. It attempts to take abstract things and establish that they are, in fact, real. At its core, ontology is the study of what is.

To make this a little more concrete, one could also say ontology is the study of what exists or is real. "Does God exist?" "Are my feelings real?", "What is 'nothing,' and does it exist?" are all examples of ontological questions. Religious ontologies consist of mentally represented assumptions about the identity and powers of stipulated supernatural entities and agencies.

The ontological argument assumes the definition of God purported by classical theism: **that God is omnipotent, omniscient, and morally perfect.** (Smith, B., 2012)

Theism is a philosophical belief in the existence of at least one deity or God. It can refer to the conception of God in classical theism, monotheism, or polytheistic religions. Theism can also include philosophical theism, which is the belief that God exists independently of any religion's teachings or revelations. Philosophical theists believe in God without doctrine, except for what can be understood through reason and natural laws.

Theism states that the existence and continuance of the universe is owed to one supreme Being, who is distinct from Creation. For this reason, theism proclaims a dualistic relation between God and the world, wherein God is a being who controls events from outside of the human world. (Bowne, 1887)

Arguments for theism fall into two main categories. Epistemic arguments, like the cosmological, ontological, and fine-tuning arguments, **conclude that God exists.** Pragmatic arguments, by contrast, conclude that **you ought to believe in God,** where 'ought' is the ought of practical rationality.

Theism is the view that there is a God who is **the creator and sustainer of the universe** and is unlimited concerning knowledge (omniscience), power (omnipotence), extension (omnipresence), and moral perfection.

The most promising argument for pro-theism is best understood as a cluster of arguments pointing to many of the purported **advantages of God's existence,** including divine intervention (**God performing miracles that help people)** and the impossibility of gratuitous evil on theism. Transpersonal ontology is built on the philosophy of creationism. (Rowe, 1986).

Creationism most often refers to belief in unique Creation: the claim that the universe and lifeforms were created as they exist today by divine action and that the only valid explanations are those compatible with a **Christian fundamentalist** literal interpretation of the creation myth.

Creationism is the belief that God created the universe, and the various life forms **out of nothing (ex nihilo**). Creationism is a theory or belief that an intelligent being, a deity, created life. This theory is built, in large part, through religious beliefs, especially that of the Bible and its story of Creation. A creationist holds to this belief and includes the many Christians, Jews, and Muslims.

The psychology of God's consciousness, or God's mind, is a complex topic that many researchers and thinkers have explored. Some adults believe that God has some human-like psychological traits, such as the ability to feel love. However, they also believe that God's mind differs from human minds in other ways, such as having more knowledge and being unable to experience emotions like embarrassment.

One scientific study suggests that a sense of God could be linked to a specific part of the brain that produces a sense of spiritual experience. The study found a gene correlated with people's spirituality, but there is opposition to the idea that spiritual consciousness can be explained solely by genes. t can be argued that there is an intimate connection between self-awareness and God-consciousness, with God-consciousness correlated negatively with the empirical self and positively with the authentic self. (Numbers, 2006)

Elohim Is The Creator. God identifies Himself as Elohim 35 times at the start of Scripture. Elohim is the only name used for God from Genesis 1:1 to Genesis 2:3. The literal translation of the name Elohim is "strong one. The term "Elohim" means "supreme one" or "mighty one." It is not only used by the one true God.; bereshith bara Elohim refers to history (there was a beginning, bereshith), then to Creation (bara, he created), and then to the Creator, Elohim. God, therefore, is a Creator and operates in real history, not in some abstract realm of man's imagination. (Baird, 1860)

In Genesis 1:26, we find the expression, 'Let us make man in our image, according to our likeness. These plurals are particularly associated with the Creation of man (1:27). The term has its roots in Genesis 1:27, wherein "God created man in his own image..." This scriptural passage does not mean that God is in human form but that humans are in the image of God in their moral, spiritual, and intellectual nature.

So, God created man in His own image; in the image of God He created him; male and female He created them. Be fruitful, multiply, fill the earth, subdue, rule. We can encapsulate these ideas by using the word abundance. Humans were made with the intent of abundant living. (Edelman, 1995).

In the Bible, Hebrews 12:9 states that God is "**the Father of spirits".** In this verse, "in subjection unto" refers to being influenced by or submitting to someone. The phrase "God of the spirits of all flesh" also appears in the Bible in Numbers 16:22 and Numbers 27:16. In

Numbers 27:16, Moses invoked "the Lord" [yhwh/Jehovah], the God [ʾĕlohê] of **the spirits of all flesh."** Numbers 16:22 reads, "O God [ʾēl], the God [ʾĕlohê] of the spirits of all flesh." In the context of Numbers 16, as it now exists, YHWH/Jehovah is clearly the ʾēl, or God, intended (see verses 19, 20, 23). God: The Supreme Father Of all Souls. Therefore, man is a tripartite being.

In Christian theology, the **tripartite view, or trichotomy,** is the idea that humans comprise three distinct parts: **body, spirit, and soul.** This view contrasts with the bipartite view, or dichotomy, which considers soul and spirit different names for the same thing. The tripartite view (trichotomy) holds that humankind is a composite of three distinct components: body, spirit, and soul.

The Bible seems to present humans as consisting of three parts: body, soul, and spirit (1 Thessalonians 5:23; Hebrews 4:12). This is called the "tripartite" nature of man. Much like the divine Trinity, the three parts of a human make one being. This model of man is the spiritual framework of our philosophy of Transpersonal Mental health care practice. (Witherington, and Ice, 2002)

Spirituality Framework: A therapy model Of Transpersonal mental health care practice that places spirituality at a person's core, depicting it as two concentric circles around a centre. In this model, the spirit is considered a person's Being, not a component, and is not harmed by illness or injury. Spiritual Well-Being Model: A model that discusses spiritual potential and spiritual health. Spiritual potential is each person's inner resources, while spiritual health uses these resources during times of stress.

The ethos of Transpersonal mental health care affirms that people are not merely physical bodies requiring mechanical fixing. Spiritual health care can help people maintain health and cope with illness, trauma, loss, and life transitions by integrating body, mind, and spirit into mental health care. (Coyle, 2002)

Our concept of spirituality is connected to a sound relationship with the creator. Developing a spiritual connection with God is similar to building a relationship with a friend or family member. It can take time and effort and involves spending time together, talking, and sharing. Prayer is not only about talking to God but also about listening.

Praying regularly can help you connect with God and understand him better. You can also try praying with a community or congregation to create a sense of unity and support. Establishing a daily or regular prayer routine can help strengthen your connection with God. It becomes a sacred time to nurture your spirituality, allowing for a deeper understanding of your faith. Developing Self-Awareness: Through prayer, you can reflect on your thoughts, actions, and intentions. This will enhance your individual spirituality. (Miner-Williams, 2006)

Transpersonal Mental health care practice is based on individual spirituality. Individual spirituality is a person's personal experience or belief in God, the creator beyond themselves. It can involve searching for meaning and purpose or believing in a supernatural realm or afterlife.

It can also include religious or cultural practices, connection with others, and self-improvement. Spirituality involves the recognition of a feeling or sense or belief that there is something greater than myself, something more to being human than sensory experience and that the greater whole of which we are part is **cosmic or divine in nature.**

Reference

- Smith, B., 2012. Ontology. In The Furniture of the World (pp. 47-68). Brill.
- Bowne, B.P., 1887. Philosophy of theism. Harper.
- Rowe, W.L., 1986. Theism. Faith and Philosophy, 3(2), pp.202-206.
- Numbers, R.L., 2006. The creationists: from scientific creationism to intelligent design (No. 33). Harvard University Press.
- Baird, S.J., 1860. The Elohim Revealed: In the Creation and Redemption of Man. Lindsay & Blakiston.
- Edelman, D.V. ed., 1995. The Triumph of Elohim: From Yahwisms to Judaisms (Vol. 13). Peeters Publishers.
- Witherington, B. and Ice, L.M., 2002. The shadow of the Almighty: Father, Son, and Spirit in Biblical perspective. Wm. B. Eerdmans Publishing.
- Coyle, J., 2002. Spirituality and health: towards a framework for exploring the relationship

between spirituality and health. Journal of Advanced Nursing, 37(6), pp.589-597.

- Miner-Williams, D., 2006. Putting a puzzle together: making spirituality meaningful for nursing using an evolving theoretical framework. Journal of Clinical Nursing, 15(7), pp.811-821.

Chapter 3- Understanding the Spiritual Nature of the Human Mind

In Christianity, the soul is a non-physical part of a person that is immortal and given by God. It is a human's spiritual element and the subject of human consciousness and freedom. The soul and body together make up a unique human nature. According to the Bible, the soul is the combination of the physical body and the life-giving spirit of God that makes up a human being.

The only Hebrew Word traditionally translated as "soul" (nephesh) in English-language Bibles refers to a living, breathing, conscious body rather than an immortal soul. (Alper, 2008).

We Are a 3-Part Whole

We are spirit, have a soul and live in a body

Christians believe that the soul is God-given and that it is immortal. Some Christians believe that only humans have souls, and this is what makes people unique and special and different from all other life forms. The soul is sometimes described as the spiritual element of humans.

The spiritual principle of human beings. The soul is the subject of human consciousness and freedom; soul and body together form one unique human nature. Each human soul is individual and immortal, immediately created by God.

According to the Bible, the soul is a person's consciousness, desires, and emotions and comprises three parts: **the mind, will, and emotions**. The Bible also suggests that the soul needs knowledge. The Bible also indicates that the soul is central to a person's identity and can be strong or unsteady, lost or saved. God's Word proves that the soul has three parts: the mind, the will, and the emotion.

The "soul," in the Bible, is a whole person with consciousness, desires and emotions. The book of Proverbs says, "The labourer's appetite works for him" (Proverbs 16:26). The Hebrew Word for "appetite" here (nephesh) can also be translated as "desires" or "needs." So, the desires of a worker's soul compel him to work. (Pribram, 2007)

In many religions and philosophies, the soul is considered a person's spiritual or immaterial essence that gives them life, individuality, and humanity. It's often seen as synonymous **with the mind or self and is sometimes believed to be immortal**. While the spirit is eternal and incorruptible, the soul is not. The soul is a link between the material body and the spiritual self and, therefore, shares some characteristics of both.

The soul can be attracted to the spiritual or the material realm, thus the **battlefield of good and evil**. Plato's tripartite soul is a theory that analyzes three parts of the soul. The parts are the rational part, the spirited part, and the appetitive part. A soul comprises the **mind, will, and emotions of a person.** The soul is the seat of feelings, desires, and affections. It's the character or substance of a person. In Hebrew (Old Testament), the Word used for soul is nepes; in Greek (New Testament), **it's psyche.**

Psychology generally approaches the concept of the soul with scepticism due to its lack of empirical evidence. However, some psychologists may study how beliefs about the soul or spiritual experiences affect mental health, well-being, and behaviour. The soul casts the experience of the **spirit into emotions** and images transmitted into personal awareness and the body, a process known as the ego-self axis.

The soul theory is one of the most popular personal identity theories, as the soul is an eternal power that does not die or break. It is, as believed by many, the only immortal part of our being. It does not age, die, or disappear. (Wein, 2014)

Soul and spirituality are words with many interpretations and can be misunderstood. In spirituality, the soul is the spiritual part of a person that is believed to give life to the body and, in many religions, is believed to live forever. It can also be defined as a person's deeply felt moral and emotional nature, or the ability to feel kindness and sympathy for others, to appreciate beauty and art, and more.

The soul comprises the mind, will, and emotions of a person. It's the seat of feelings, desires, and affections, and it's the character or substance of a person. There are three powers of the soul: the intellect, the will, and the senses. The spirit can also directly affect the soul through deep emotional, psychological, or moral feelings such as love (1 John 4:7-21; Galatians 5:22-24; Colossians 1:7-8).

Soul health refers to the spiritual health and well-being of an individual. There are three essential aspects of soul health. They include soul-searching, soul care or nurture, and soul flourishing. Soul searching is deep and conscious introspection of one's emotions and motives. A healthy soul is full of Joy and gratitude. Emotional resilience. Kindness and compassion toward others.

A sense of purpose and connection to God is more significant than yourself. Symptoms of positive soul health: joy, compassion, peace, trust in God's goodness, creativity, a sense of humour, generosity toward others, clear understanding of vision, intimacy with others, energy for work and play, a desire to connect with God. Proverbs 2:10 gives us the **spiritual ground** to prove that the mind is a part of the soul.

The mind is spiritual. The essence of the human mind, with its true nature, is a spiritual entity. This fundamental assumption is very crucial to the practice of transpersonal mental health care. The concept of body, mind, and spirit is that people are more than just their thoughts; their bodies, emotions, and spirituality combine to make them who they are. These factors can also determine health and identity. The central concept behind the mind-body-spirit connection is that we are all more than just our thoughts. We are also our bodies, our emotions, and our spirituality. All these things combine to give us identity, determine our mental health, and make us who we are.

Transpersonal mental health care purports that the state of the spiritual health of the mind affects our mental health. Thoughts are spiritual in nature and origin. However, there are psycho-somatic stimuli that initiate thoughts. The union of the body and spirit defines the human person. The human person is an embodied spirit. We are all more than just our thoughts. We are also our bodies, our emotions, and our spirituality. Conventional psychology completely denied the spiritual nature of the mind. Their psychological interventions are based on the foundation of the neuro-psychology of the human brain.

Neuropsychology is a branch of psychology that studies how the brain and nervous system relate to a person's behaviour and cognition. On the contrary, transpersonal neuropsychology believes that the spirit of the man can influence his cognition. (Kumar, 2004)

Transpersonal neuropsychology is grounded in transpersonal psychology. A legitimate branch of psychology that investigates the nature of human experience, spiritual development, and the connection between the self and a higher plane of existence. The argument is that our thoughts are spiritual and that spiritual interference can impact one's thinking, leading to behaviour which can be damaging or good depending on the spiritual health of the soul that accommodates the mind.

Proverbs 4:23 says we should guard our heart with all diligence because from out of it flows the issues of life. This scripture implies that whatever we allow to enter our hearts, if not examined and evaluated correctly, will undoubtedly be expressed in our lives and our actions – in positive or negative ways. This is the definition of **Transpersonal cognitive psychology.**

(Piedmont, and Wilkins, 2019)

Transpersonal cognitive psychology. Cognitive psychology is the scientific study of how people think, learn, remember, and perceive events. It focuses on mental processes like attention, creativity, language, memory, problem-solving, reasoning, and understanding. Cognitive psychology is the branch of psychology dedicated to studying how people think. The cognitive perspective in psychology focuses on how the interactions of thinking, emotion, creativity, and problem-solving abilities affect how and why you think the way you do—however, **Transpersonal cognitive psychology** is the scientific study of how our spiritual -self affects our thinking and behaviour.

The psychology of spirituality is a branch of psychology that studies the connection between human **spirituality and mental health**. Spirituality can be defined as a quality that seeks inspiration, meaning, purpose, and reverence, even in people who don't believe in God. It can also mean being connected, self-aware, authentic, and searching for higher values and inner freedom.

Your higher self is the part of you unencumbered by ego and the divisions it can stoke between you and your fellow humans. It's the non-material dimension of you (**some call it a soul or spirit)** that's part of the cosmic or celestial whole. The spiritual health of your higher self, also known as your **spirit man,** is the focus of transpersonal mental health care practice. (Wein, 2014)

Spiritual health is a broad term that refers to a person's connection to God, the divine creator, such as a higher purpose, a community, or a calling. It can also include a person's values, beliefs, and morals that give them a sense of meaning in their life. Spiritually healthy people may have a strong sense of purpose and feel able to integrate meaning into their lives. They may also be able to look at obstacles as opportunities and make peace with their lives. The discovery of a Higher purpose from God, the divine creator, that is the reason for your existence, is the foundation for sound spiritual health.

Reference

- Alper, Matthew. The" God" part of the brain: A scientific interpretation of human spirituality and God. Sourcebooks, Inc., 2008.
- Pribram, K., 2007. Quantum information processing in brain systems and the spiritual nature of mankind. Frontier Perspectives, 16(1), pp.4-12.
- Kumar, S., 2004. The Spiritual Imperative. Song, p.202.
- Wein, S., 2014. Spirituality—the psyche or the soul?. Palliative & Supportive Care, 12(2), pp.91-94.
- Piedmont, R.L. and Wilkins, T.A., 2019. Understanding the psychological soul of

spirituality: A guidebook for research and practice. Routledge.

- Wein, S., 2014. Spirituality—the psyche or the soul?. Palliative & Supportive Care, 12(2), pp.91-94.

Chapter 4- Understanding the Principles of Eternal Purpose of Life.

There is one answer to whether Life has a purpose. The purpose of your Life exists in the Mind of the Divine creator. Your life purpose consists of the central motivating aims of your Life—the reasons you get up in the morning. Purpose can guide life decisions, influence behaviour, shape goals, offer a sense of direction, and create meaning. For some people, purpose is connected to vocation—meaningful, satisfying work. God tells Jeremiah, "Before I formed you in the womb, I knew you."

This means I've known you before there was you to be known by anyone else. Before you were in the womb, I knew you before I even began to form you there. Knew you, who you were, what you would do. Jeremiah 1:5 states that before Jeremiah was born, even before he was formed in his mother's womb, the Lord had specific plans for his Life. Scholars widely interpret this passage to mean that God predestined the course of Jeremiah's Life. (Ozkaptan, 2008).

Scripture credits God with creating children long before they are physically born. David addresses God as having formed his inner being before birth. Job says something similar: "You clothed me with skin and flesh, and knit me together with bones and sinews" (Job 10:11). Just as you do not know the way and path of the wind or how the bones are formed in the womb of a pregnant woman, even so, you do not know the activity of God who makes all things. Ecclesiastes 11:5-6 Amplified Bible (AMP). Because God is omniscient, He knows everyone before their conception and birth.

He knows those who are His and those who are not; He isn't bound by time. Before Jeremiah was born, He appointed Jeremiah to be His prophet and appointed him to be God's messenger to the people. This election is said to take place "before the foundation of the world" (cf. John 17:24; 1 Pet. 1:20). That is, God's choice in election occurred before time and creation, emphasizing that this choice was based on God's sovereign purpose, not human merits. (Cho, 2020)

God is a God of Purpose: **He Created all things for His Will to Fulfill His Purpose**. Our God is a God of purpose, and He created all things for His will so that He might accomplish His will and fulfill it (see Rev. 4:11; Eph. 3:9-11). God's plan for people's lives, also known as the plan of salvation, **gives meaning and purpose to Life on Earth.** This plan answers questions like "Where did I come from?", "Why am I here?" and "What happens after I die?". God, our loving Heavenly Father, wants us to find happiness and joy. He created a plan for us to grow, live by faith, and return to live with Him someday.

His plan gives meaning and context to our Life here on Earth. There are things that God will show us through prayer, and we can learn no other way. Jeremiah 33:3 says, "Call to me, and I will answer you and tell you great and unsearchable things you do not know" (NIV). You can't find your God-given purpose without consulting God through prayer. (Cho, 2020).

The psychology of purpose is the idea that a sense of purpose in Life is a psychological construct that can lead to positive development and well-being. It can also help people avoid negative experiences and behaviours and achieve higher levels. According to the psychological literature, purpose is a stable intention to accomplish something personally meaningful and positively impact the world. It's more than a temporary motivational state, and it's not an accomplishment with a terminal outcome.

Instead, it's a self-organizing life aim that you're looking forward to and working towards, like a gaze that stays in front of you as you move forward. The purpose of Life is a stable and generalized intention to accomplish something personally meaningful while leading to productive engagement with some aspect of the world beyond the self. (McKnight and Kashdan, 2009).

Having a meaningful target to direct one's efforts may contribute to a sense of optimism and hope. Individuals who lead lives of purpose are more likely to report high levels of life satisfaction than others. Purpose theory is a prima facie attractive account of what could make a life meaningful. It spells out what it would mean to **'exist for a reason'** or **'life to have a point'**. Research suggests that having a purpose in Life can improve mental health, including reducing depression and anxiety and building resilience after adverse events.

This association is influential for clinical populations. Research indicates that having a purpose in Life is good for mental health. For example, having a greater purpose in Life was significantly associated with lower levels of depression and anxiety. Studies have indicated a link between purpose-driven living and a reduced risk of mental health issues. Whether it's depression, anxiety, or existential angst, **having a clear sense of purpose can act as a preventative measure.**

Experiencing a lack of purpose, you may feel constantly bored, dissatisfied or empty, like Life has no meaning. You may feel unfulfilled in your relationships with others, disaffected at home and work, and anxiously ruminating on the point of Life. Lack of direction/purpose could contribute to anxiety/depression; experiencing depression/anxiety could contribute to less motivation and participation in things that used to give purpose, or they could compound each other. Past traumatic experiences can also contribute to lacking purpose and meaning. If you've been through difficult times in your Life, it can be hard to see beyond the pain or trauma. Negative life experiences such as divorce, the death of a loved one, or job loss can also leave us feeling empty and devoid of meaning. (Wong, 2014)

Spirituality can help people find purpose and meaning in their lives. It can also help people cope with stress, depression, and anxiety and develop a more hopeful outlook on Life. Spiritual well-being is the ability to establish meaning and find purpose through the

connection to our Divine maker, Who can only reveal our reason for existence and a sense of connection beyond the self. It can benefit our overall well-being by cultivating our sense of inner understanding and place in Life. Transpersonal mental health care believes Spirituality involves the recognition of a feeling or sense or belief that there is something greater than myself, something more to being human than sensory experience, and that the greater whole of which we are part is cosmic or divine.

You can find purpose in Spirituality by Posing a significant spiritual question that you'd like to explore or be more knowledgeable about. Who is this God I believe in? How do I make sense of evil in the world and live with that? What is prayer? Respond by reflecting, meditating, or writing in your journal, and answer it through your life story.

The basis of Transpersonal Mental Health care practice is discovering a sense of meaningfulness in your Life and **knowing that you have a purpose to fulfill.** Many factors define Spirituality, such as religious faith, beliefs, values, ethics, principles, and morals. **Spiritual purpose is** about establishing a set of values, principles and beliefs that give Life meaning to you, and then using them to guide your decisions and actions. You can embark on a journey towards a more satisfying life by cultivating positive emotions, building meaningful relationships, finding purpose, and prioritizing well-being. In transpersonal mental health care practice philosophy and psychology, self-fulfilment is realizing one's most profound spiritual vision for existence and capacities.

In conclusion, finding spiritual purpose leads to spiritual well-being. Spiritual well-being can have many health benefits, including **improved mental health,** physical health, and longevity. Spiritual well-being can help people develop a sense of purpose and meaning, which can help them deal with Life's challenges. It can also help people cultivate motivation, peace, and **self-worth** and improve their ability to handle stress.

Spirituality can also provide a foundation for building hope and **self-esteem** and give people tools to self-advocate. According to the Mayo Clinic, people who practice Spirituality tend to live longer and have a lower risk of cardiovascular disease and hypertension. They may also be more likely to exercise, eat well, and attend preventive screenings. Spirituality can help people cope with physical or emotional pain and promote close family and friendship bonds. It can also create a supportive community that offers safe social engagement and a sense of belonging.

Reference

- Ozkaptan, H., 2008. Life's Purpose-Development of Your Living and Eternal Spirit. Lulu. com.
- Cho, D.D., 2020. The Covenant Life: Find Your God-Given Purpose in Life. Wipf and Stock Publishers.

- McKnight, P.E. and Kashdan, T.B., 2009. Purpose in Life as a system that creates and sustains health and well-being: An integrative, testable theory. Review of General Psychology, 13(3), pp.242-251.
- Wong, P.T., 2014. Viktor Frankl's meaning-seeking model and positive psychology. Meaning in positive and existential psychology, pp.149-184.

Chapter 5- The Transpersonal Mental Health Practitioner Framework

Our Transpersonal Mental Health Practitioner Framework is underpinned by the three components of spiritual health: **Religious, Individualistic, and Material world-oriented.**

The religious components may result from human connection with God, including a sense of relationship with God, love, prayer, the feeling that God is practical and God-oriented knowledge, attitude, and behaviours. The individualistic component comes from the human connection with himself. Instances include self-scrutiny, examining the meaning of life, hope, self-actualization, moral virtues, peace, responsibility for oneself, balance, transcendence, values, mysticism, culture, knowledge, attitude, and behaviours related to oneself. (Bensley, 1991).

The Material World-Oriented Component refers to the human connection with others and nature. Connection with others creates a sense of responsibility toward them, unconditional love, forgiveness, pacifism, harmony, knowledge, attitude, and behaviours concerning others. Spiritual health can be defined as the overall health of a person's soul, values, beliefs, and purpose. It can be a unique journey of self-discovery and growth for each person. Some say spiritual health can be complicated, but its common characteristics can describe it. These characteristics include organized religion, prayer, hope, purpose, and peace. The transpersonal mental health care practice operates according to the bio-psychosocial spiritual framework.

The biopsychosocial-spiritual model is a holistic framework that considers the interactions between a person's biological, psychological, social, and spiritual aspects. It's often used in clinical settings, especially for patients with life-threatening illnesses. The model views people as beings in relationships and illness as a disruptive force in their biological relationships. It also recognizes that each aspect of a person can be affected by their history and disease and that each element can interact and affect other aspects. (Hawks,1994).

The model was initially developed by George L. Engel (1913–1999), a prominent scholar in the psychosomatic movement. It's since expanded to include a spiritual component, acknowledging that spiritual well-being can significantly impact mental health and quality of life. The " spiritual " concept is broad and fluid and can refer to many different aspects, from individual spirituality based on theism and deeply religious experiences.

A biopsychosocial-spiritual model is a holistic approach that acknowledges the interaction between physical, psychological, social, and spiritual aspects of patient care and well-being (Beng, 2004). Exploration of a client's spiritual beliefs and how they influence their mental health. Support that respects and aligns with the patient's spiritual perspective. Discussion of meditation, mindfulness, and prayer. Encourage connections with spiritual communities.

The spiritual-mental health counselling approach combines counselling modalities, such as cognitive-behavioural and psychodynamic therapy, with spiritual practices, such as meditation and prayer. It aims to help individuals integrate their spiritual beliefs and practices into their well-being. (Saad, De Medeiros, and Mosini, 2017).

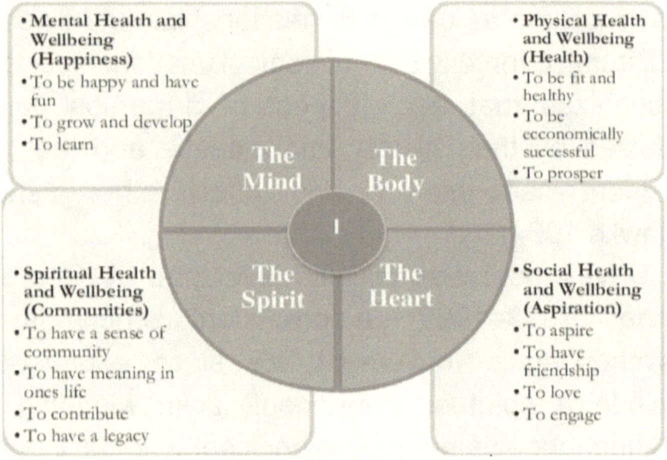

Counsellors often discuss forgiveness, justice, suffering, doubt, joy, hope, love, and grace with their clients. Spiritual counsellors are also trained in techniques such as prayer or guided imagery, which can further assist a person in finding the deeper meaning in life. Clients can find clarity and answers to the following **5 Questions of life.**

- Who am I? – Identity
- Where did I come from? – Your Eternal Origin

- Why am I here on earth? – Finding Your Purpose
- What can I do? – Finding Your True Potential
- Where am I going in life? – Your life Vision Based on Your Divine Assignment

Transpersonal mental health care practice uses Psychoeducation, which involves learning about and understanding mental health and well-being. It's similar to physical education, where you learn about how your body works, how to look after it and the impacts of different strains or stressors - but instead, you apply this to your mental health. Psychoeducation, an organized process of imparting information about illness to sufferers, their families, and sometimes to staff members, is an element of virtually all types of therapy.

Transpersonal Counselling uses various techniques to help clients explore their spiritual selves and create meaning. The goal of transpersonal therapy is to help people transcend their current view of themselves and open their minds to new ways of approaching challenges. Transpersonal therapists may use techniques from both Eastern traditions and Western psychology. A transpersonal therapist may draw from various religions and spiritual practices for tools and methods to help you explore areas of your consciousness not typically accessed and use your spirituality to guide you through troubled times. (Shorrock, 2007)

The transpersonal mental health care model integrates the spiritual, social, emotional, intellectual, physical, and creative being into one complete element and addresses the **five questions of life** for mental health treatment. Transpersonal mental health care is a therapy that focuses on **healing one's Spirit rather than the body or mind.** Transpersonal mental health care primarily focuses on healing and integrating the splits and inner divisions that occur through social and cultural conditioning among the physical, emotional, cognitive, and spiritual aspects of a person's being. (Shorrock, 2007)

Transpersonal mental health care will draw from diverse techniques, which will be taught and supported in a way that clients can continue to apply beyond therapy. These techniques will be tailored to each client's needs and circumstances. The core guiding principle of Transpersonal mental health care counselling is a client-centred approach.

Client-centred therapy, also known as person-centred or Rogerian therapy, is a humanistic approach to Counselling that gives clients an active role in directing their treatment. The client is considered the expert in their life and leads the direction of Counselling. The therapist's role is to create a supportive environment where clients can explore and understand their feelings.

The therapist avoids giving advice or implementing strategies, instead using techniques like active listening, reflection of feelings, open questions, and paraphrasing. The therapist focuses on the client's subjective Understanding of their situation rather than their interpretation. The therapist treats the client with kindness, compassion, and Understanding and helps them realize their own resources and support. (Law, Baptiste, and Mills,1995)

Client-centred therapy can be used to treat a variety of issues, including relationship problems, depression, anxiety, grief, addictions, sexuality, anger, and difficult life transitions. It's ideal for people motivated by self-discovery and want to solve their problems. The fundamental principles of person-centred care are treating patients with dignity and respect, encouraging participation in decision-making, and communicating with patients about their clinical condition and treatment options. Empathetic Understanding: the client-centred therapist must extend empathy to the client to form a positive therapeutic relationship and act as a mirror, reflecting the client's thoughts and feelings, allowing the client to understand them better. (Law, Baptiste, and Mills,1995)

Transpersonal mental health care adopts Christian Counselling, and the Holy Spirit is believed to play a role in the counselling process. The Holy Spirit can help people understand themselves and others. Transpersonal mental health care Counsellors should maintain spiritual discipline and keep under the anointing of the Holy Spirit. Besides the Holy Spirit's power, Counselling lacks healing power. The Holy Spirit guides us into all the truth. Takes the things of the Lord Jesus Christ and discloses them to us. The Holy Spirit takes the realities of our Wonderful Counselor and makes them our possession to walk in. Spiritual therapy delves into the core of **negative thoughts** and progressively helps one develop a more healthy thought process. As our spiritual guru, the Holy Spirit awakens awareness of one's conscious thoughts and helps shift the mind into positivity. (Falaye, 2013)

The Holy Spirit is **the Lord and Giver of Life** in the Nicene Creed. He is the Creator Spirit, present before the creation of the universe and through **his power,** everything was made in Jesus Christ by God the Father. The Holy Spirit's healing power can extend to the **mind and body** and manifest in various ways. The Holy Spirit can help people heal from addictions through therapy and recovery groups. The Holy Spirit's healing power is different from the healing that comes from medical intervention and is instead a supernatural gift. It also extends to the mind and the body. We believe the Holy Spirit still heals people today – sometimes through miracles, sometimes through medicine, and often through the combination of modern medicine and the healing power of the Holy Spirit. (Falaye, 2013).

Reference

- Bensley, R.J., 1991. Defining spiritual health: A review of the literature. Journal of Health Education, 22(5), pp.287-290.
- Hawks, S., 1994. Spiritual health: Definition and theory. Wellness perspectives, 10(4).
- Saad, M., De Medeiros, R. and Mosini, A.C., 2017. Are we ready for a true biopsychosocial–spiritual model? The many

meanings of "spiritual". Medicines, 4(4), p.79.

- Shorrock, A., 2007. The transpersonal in psychology, psychotherapy and Counselling. Springer.
- Law, M., Baptiste, S. and Mills, J., 1995. Client-centred practice: what does it mean, and does it make a difference? Canadian Journal of Occupational Therapy, 62(5), pp.250-257.
- Falaye, A.O., 2013. Counselling from the Christian point of view: religious psychotherapy. IFE PsychologIA: An International Journal, 21(3), pp.54-61.

Chapter 6- Transpersonal Cognitive Subjective Epistemology.

Epistemology is the theory of knowledge. It is concerned with the mind's relation to reality. What is it for this relation to be one of knowledge? Do we know things? And if we do, how and when do we know things? Cognitive psychology studies internal mental processes—all of the workings inside your brain, including perception, thinking, memory, attention, language, problem-solving, and learning. A big problem for cognitive psychologists is that measuring internal processes such as attention and perception is difficult.

Instead of measuring these processes directly, cognitive psychologists use tests that **measure behaviours** or **external features** that they believe are related to the internal process. Empiricism is a philosophical belief that knowledge is based on experience, **particularly sensory experiences.** In psychology, it's a way of knowing that emphasizes the role of observation and experience in acquiring knowledge. Empiricists believe that learning is based on perception and observations and that knowledge is impossible without experience. The term comes from the Greek word empeiria, which means experience. (Hanohano, 1999)

A sensory experience is a conscious experience that occurs when a person sees, hears, touches, smells, or tastes something. The human senses can categorize sensory experiences, such as visual (seeing colour and light) or auditory (hearing sounds, music, and speech). Some say that the most memorable experiences engage more than one sense. Sensory experiences are the experiences we have when we see, hear, touch, smell, or taste something.

They provide topics for the **theory of knowledge** and the philosophy of mind. The theory of knowledge concerns how experiences yield knowledge of the world about us. Empiricism is the idea that all learning comes from experience and observations. The term empiricism comes from the Greek word for experience: empeiria. The theory of Empiricism attempts to explain how human beings acquire knowledge and improve their conceptual understanding of the world. (Buker, 2003)

Empiricism is a method that emphasizes observation and experience in the pursuit of knowledge. It has several limitations. Empiricism is subjective because it relies on people's observations and can only provide information about what people can observe. For example, Empiricism may be limited in understanding objects in space or at a small scale that people cannot observe. Empirical research may oversimplify complex phenomena, mainly relying solely on quantitative methods. These methods may struggle to capture the nuances of specific social, cultural, or psychological contexts.

Subjective reality is the idea that something is real depending on the mind and is influenced by a person's biases, emotions, **perceptions,** opinions, imagination, and conscious experience. For example, if one person finds the weather pleasant, and another finds it too hot, both views are subjective. Subjective (Individual) reality means that something is actual depending on the mind. Something subjective is based on personal opinions and feelings rather than facts. Spirituality in psychology

Subjective epistemology is a branch of philosophy that studies how individuals and communities create knowledge and meaning. It's based on the idea that how people perceive and understand the world determines what they know and that it's impossible to separate the subject from the object. Subjectivists believe that each person perceives and observes the world differently and that their beliefs are rational if they meet the standards of their community or recognized experts.

In research, Subjectivism epistemology studies individual behaviour, perceptions, and feelings of uncertainty. It allows for applying probability calculus to personal experiences and views knowledge as specific to an individual rather than an objective event. Religious ontologies consist of mentally represented assumptions about the identity and powers of stipulated supernatural entities and agencies. (Hartelius, 2007)

Spiritual ontologies consist of mentally represented assumptions about the identity and powers of stipulated supernatural entities and agencies. Such representations seem culturally specific, and it is often assumed that their variability is unbounded. Spiritual reality differs from objective reality in that it refers to the existence **of God as a transcendent creator or ruler of the universe.** The spiritual reality may be considered the ultimate meaning-maker for all that exists. The human sense of a spiritual reality is present in all known cultures. Transpersonal psychology is based on spiritual philosophy, which refers to any philosophy or teaching pertaining to spirituality. It may incorporate religious or esoteric themes. It can include any belief or thought system that embraces the existence of a reality that **cannot be physically perceived.** (Thayer, 2017).

Spiritual perception is the ability to experience God or God-related phenomena directly, without inference, and in a way that's similar to the bodily senses. It can also refer to the ability to see and recognize spiritual truth or to see what others can't. Spiritual perception is our subconscious gathering of information from the Spiritual Realm. Once you reach a certain level of spiritual enlightenment, your spiritual awareness is tremendously enhanced, and **intuition (your spiritual perception in a dormant state)** is activated or awakened and thus transformed through transpersonal development.

We all experience stimuli in the environment (in the physical world) differently through our physical and sensory systems (sight, sound, touch, taste, smell, etc.). While simultaneously gathering information from our **spiritual sensory system.** We possess a "mirror "or "shadow" sense for every physical sense we possess.

The conscious mind perceives the Physical Realm, while the subconscious mind perceives the Spiritual Realm. Even how we process these "stimuli" varies from person to person. This means that we all experience spiritual perception differently. Consequently, each spiritual perception, or "shadow sense", manifests differently for each person. The Dictionary of Bible Themes defines spiritual perception as seeing beneath the outward form to the underlying, often hidden, reality. (Stranahan, 2001)

Spiritual knowledge is a field of research that explores the meaning of existence, our connection to the universe, and our values in society and organizations. It can also help us understand more profound questions about our existence, such as who we are, why we are here, and why we die. Spiritual knowledge is considered the third component of the triple helix of knowledge. It's an integral part of spiritual intelligence and spiritual capital and can help us discover the value of what's essential in life and see meaning in the world around us. Some say that spiritual knowing is a unitary transformative pattern of knowing the world and can create a feeling of alignment with a universal world of goodness. Spiritual knowledge is about the deep human concerns of our existence and our connection with the universe. (Bratianu, 2015).

Transpersonal Cognitive Subjective Epistemology lies within the paradigm of spiritual knowledge. Spiritual psychology is an area of psychology that seeks to integrate the spiritual and transcendent aspects of the human experience within the framework of modern psychology. A biopsychosocial-spiritual model is a holistic approach acknowledging the interaction between physical, psychological, social, and spiritual aspects of patient care and well-being. It's primarily about believing in God and actively participating in organized spirituality of religion. For others, it's about non-religious experiences that help them connect with their spiritual selves through quiet reflection, time in nature, private prayer or meditation.

Transpersonal Cognitive psychology goes beyond the individual's subjective experiences to include the influences of **spiritual and transcendent experiences.** Transpersonal cognitive psychology concerns end that transcend personal identity and immediate desires. It seeks to understand how the connection between the self and higher consciousness can lead to growth and self-development. Transpersonal Cognitive psychology Investigates non-ordinary states of consciousness, such as those experienced during meditation, after ingesting psychedelics, or during peak performance, such as optimal flow, as well as spiritual or religious experiences and mystical states.

Reference

- Hanohano, P., 1999. The spiritual imperative of Native epistemology: Restoring harmony and balance to Education. Canadian Journal of Native Education, 23(2).

- Buker, B., 2003. Spiritual development and the epistemology of systems theory. Journal of Psychology and Theology, 31(2), pp.143-153.
- Hartelius, G., 2007. Quantitative somatic phenomenology: Toward an epistemology of subjective. Journal of Consciousness Studies, 14(12), pp.24-56.
- Thayer-Bacon, B.J., 2017. Teaching Spirituality as Ontology in Public Schools. A Response to" Democratic Foundations of Spiritual Responsive Pedagogy". Democracy and Education, 25(1), p.13.
- Stranahan, S., 2001. Spiritual perception, attitudes about spiritual care, and spiritual care practices among nurse practitioners. Western Journal of Nursing Research, 23(1), pp.90-104.
- Bratianu, C., 2015. Spiritual knowledge. Organizational knowledge dynamics: Managing knowledge creation, acquisition, sharing, and transformation, pp.72-102.

Chapter 7- Transpersonal Cognitive Behavioural Therapy- TCBT

Cognitive behavioural therapy (CBT) combines cognitive therapy and behavioural therapy to help people manage problems by changing their thoughts and behaviour. CBT is based on the idea that our thoughts, feelings, and behaviours are closely linked and influence each other. **CBT aims to help people recognize unhelpful patterns and break them down to approach problems differently and improve their feelings**. CBT can also be used to treat physical conditions such as chronic pain, tinnitus, and rheumatism.

It can also help people cope with divorce or break-ups, grief or loss, insomnia, low self-esteem, relationship problems, and stress management. Cognitive behaviour therapy (CBT) is a type of psychotherapy. It may help you to change unhelpful or unhealthy ways of thinking, feeling, and behaving. CBT uses practical self-help strategies. These are designed to improve your quality of life immediately. CBT can be an effective way to treat depression and anxiety. (Muench, et al, 2022).

CBT may not be suitable for people with complex **mental health needs**, learning difficulties, or who dislike structure. CBT's focus on the present may also make it less practical for addressing **underlying causes of mental health** conditions, such as past experiences. Some critics argue that because CBT only addresses current problems and focuses on specific issues, it does not address the possible underlying causes of mental health conditions, such as an unhappy childhood Trauma. CBT focuses on the individual's capacity to change themselves (**their thoughts, feelings and behaviours).** It does not address broader problems in systems or families that often significantly impact an individual's health and well-being. (Hick, and Chan,2010)

Transpersonal Cognitive Behavioural Therapy

Unlike most forms of psychotherapy that concentrate on improving mental health alone, TCBT addresses mental, physical, social, emotional, creative, and intellectual needs, emphasizing the role of **a healthy spirit in healing.** TCBT is primarily focused on healing and integrating the splits and inner divisions that occur through social and cultural conditioning among the physical, emotional, mental, and spiritual aspects of a person's being (Vaughan, 1993). TCBT is an enhanced spiritual connection, greater empathy for others, and a heightened appreciation of life. These benefits extend to more specific areas of growth and healing depending on the variation of techniques used in therapy. (Hutton, 1993)

Transpersonal Cognitive Psychology studies the spiritual and transcendental aspects of the human experience, including the relationship between the mind and body, consciousness, and human transformation. It's also known as spiritual cognitive psychology. Transpersonal psychology is similar to the humanistic approach, but it goes beyond the individual's subjective experiences to include the influence of spiritual experiences. Life-changing spiritual experiences fuel religious/spiritual attitudes and behaviours, and their impact may be more profound if experienced at a younger age.

Cultivating spirituality in one's behaviour requires a complete purification of mind, body and soul, including emotional components of compassion, empathy and humanity. Spirituality influences many decisions that people make. It encourages people to have better relationships with others and the unknown. Spirituality can help you deal with stress by giving you peace, purpose, and forgiveness. The influence of spiritual experiences on cognitions is the basis of transpersonal cognitive psychology. A large body of research suggests that spiritual attachment generally benefits people. It is correlated with better **health habits** such as less smoking and drinking, an enhanced ability to cope with stress, and increased social support. (Hutton, 1993)

The Human spirits can affect our **thoughts and feelings** in several ways. Our conscious spirits move in and out of auras influenced by the spirits around us. These auras can affect our moods and thoughts and may even cause anxiety. Theta brainwave activity **can receive input from the spirit level, which can come from God or the enemy.** From God, the input can be a work of the Holy Spirit that leads, directs, and corrects us.

From the enemy, the input can be temptation or self-serving thoughts. This input comes in the form of pictures, thoughts, and impressions. Spirit can affect your emotions because everything in existence is energy, vibration and frequency. Even though we do not see it, we **FEEL it.** Depending on what we feel, it can affect our internal state. It is not always seen; however, we do **FEEL it. Our thoughts create our feelings, and our feelings drive our behaviour. (Wein, 2014)**

Our thoughts can receive input from the spirit level, which can come from God or Evil Spirits. These thoughts create feelings that drive our behaviour. This is the foundation principle of Transpersonal cognitive behavioural therapy. Conventional cognitive psychology lacks the framework to explain the influence of the spiritual world on human thoughts. Thoughts and emotions have a profound effect on one another. Thoughts can trigger emotions (worrying about an upcoming job interview may cause fear) and also serve as an appraisal of that emotion ("This isn't a realistic fear"). In addition, how we attend to and appraise our lives affects how we feel. The spiritual world's influence can trigger thoughts and emotions that lead to specific behaviours. (Wein, 2014)

A spiritual stronghold in the mind is a way of thinking and feeling that has become a fortress for negative thoughts and demonic forces. It can be a lie that Satan establishes in a person's thinking or a way of relating to life that's controlled by negative thoughts. Strongholds can be hard to detect and remove because they are buried deep in the subconscious mind and can become stronger the more they are fed. A spiritual stronghold is a habitual thought pattern built into one's thought life. Satan and his minions want to capture the minds of people, knowing that the mind is the citadel of the soul. Examples of spiritual strongholds are depression, unbelief, bad temper, resentment, worthlessness, jealousy, bitterness, unforgiveness, hatred, and anger.

Strongholds can develop over time as people interact with their environment. They can be strengthened by repeatedly establishing self-worship and disregarding God's existence in their ontology. However, strongholds can be torn down with the help of the power of the Holy -Spirit. For example, one person says that Biblical Psychology counselling helped them to see themselves as God sees them and to accept that they are loved and do not need to earn God's favour.

Spiritual strongholds are the habitual lies, thoughts, spirit blocks, and exaggerated attitudes within one's self that try to set oneself up against God. Spiritual strongholds are often seen as demons and unclean spirits that require deliverance, but most times, the warfare is within ourselves. You will need to pray to **God through the Holy Spirit** to break strongholds from the past. Then, ask the Holy Spirit to reveal any sin you need to confess and renounce. Write each one down on paper, confess it as a sin, and renounce all involvement. (Greenwood, R,2015)

Transpersonal Cognitive Behavioural Therapy invokes the Power of The Holy Spirit during therapy sessions. In Biblical Psychology **2 Corinthians 10:3-5,** a stronghold refers to a mental block. Paul is talking about arguments set up against the knowledge and truth of God. This is a mental battle. According to Biblical psychology, we need to Destroy these strongholds. Exposure to ordinary talking therapy does not destroy these strongholds.

We use God's mighty weapons**, the Power of The Holy Spirit, not worldly weapons,** to knock down the strongholds of human reasoning and to destroy false arguments in the mind. Once you recognize the stronghold, repentance is the next step to bringing it down. Be honest before God, and humbly let the Holy Spirit expose the stronghold in the darkness of your thoughts and life. Strongholds are Arguments raised against the knowledge of God. Lofty opinions that are raised against the **knowledge of God.**

Spiritual resilience comes from God's grace, renewal, and presence. God's grace allows people to overcome their fears and find true resilience. Prayer and seeking solace in God's presence are pillars of spiritual strength. Reading the Scriptures for guidance and encouragement can strengthen the Spirit. For example, Psalm 23 assures believers that God is with them even in the valley of the shadow of death. People should put their confidence in God, not in people, institutions, or the government. They can do this by listening to the Lord, staying attuned to **His Spirit,** and discerning His direction for their lives. This learned and continual process reflects a process of cumulative spiritual resilience.

God's manifest presence During therapy is when God chooses to reveal himself in our lives, making it clear and convincing that he is with us. God's omnipresence is the attribute of being everywhere at once, even when we don't experience his presence or recognize him. Manifest means to cause to be seen, displayed, made known, or revealed. God's manifest presence is what believers see and what they know and learn of God. If you are to know God, you have to get a revelation.

It is good to know about God, but He wants us to know of Him for ourselves during the therapy session. Experiencing Pentecost during therapy sessions, only those in the upper room came into contact with His manifest presence. His presence came as a rushing wind, tongues of fire, and the supernatural experience of speaking in tongues. Indeed, God showed up!. The Spirit's manifest presence is where God makes himself known to us.

This is when the indwelling Spirit uniquely and manifestly visits **during therapy.** The Holy Spirit manifests its presence in a person's life through the unique abilities it distributes and **then energizes.** These abilities are commonly known as the gifts of the Spirit. Biblical Psychology Isaiah 10:27 says, "On that day, God will remove the burden from your shoulder and destroy the yoke on your neck because of the anointing". (Del Colle, 2001)

Isaiah 10:27 defines the anointing as God's burden-removing, yoke-destroying power. The anointing is what delivers God's people and sets the captives free. The anointing is God on flesh doing what flesh can't do. It is God's supernatural that has added to our nature. Using music therapy during the session, we invoke the burden-removing, yoke-destroying power of the Holy Spirit.

Reference

- Muench, A., Vargas, I., Grandner, M.A., Ellis, J.G., Posner, D., Bastien, C.H., Drummond, S.P. and Perlis, M.L., 2022. We know CBT-I works. Now what?. Faculty reviews, 11.
- Hick, S.F. and Chan, L., 2010. Mindfulness-based cognitive therapy for depression: effectiveness and limitations. Social Work in Mental Health, 8(3), pp.225-237.
- Hutton, M.S., 1993. Spiritual beliefs, spiritual practices, psychotherapeutic techniques and personality types among transpersonal, cognitive-behavioural, and psychoanalytic psychotherapists. California Institute of Integral Studies.
- Wein, S., 2014. Spirituality—the psyche or the soul?. Palliative & Supportive Care, 12(2), pp.91-94.
- Greenwood, R., 2015. Defeating Strongholds of the Mind: A Believer's Guide to Breaking Free. Charisma Media.

- Del Colle, R., 2001. The Holy Spirit: Presence, Power, Person. Theological Studies, 62(2), pp.322-340.

Chapter 8- Transpersonal Approach to Dealing with Depression

Depression

Depression is a constant feeling of sadness and loss of interest, which stops you from doing your normal activities. Different types of Depression exist, with symptoms ranging from relatively minor to severe. Generally, Depression does not result from a single event but a mix of events and factors. Feelings of sadness, tearfulness, emptiness or hopelessness.

Angry outbursts, irritability or frustration, even over small matters. Loss of interest or pleasure in most or all normal activities, such as sex, hobbies or sports. Sleep disturbances, including insomnia or sleeping too much. **Feelings of hopelessness, worthlessness, or helplessness.** Loss of interest or pleasure in hobbies and activities. Fatigue, lack of energy, or feeling slowed down. Difficulty concentrating, remembering, or making decisions. (Beck, and Alford, 2009)

Root Cause Of Depression

According to the World Health Organization, Depression is caused by a complex combination of biological, psychological, and social factors. Research suggests there's unlikely to be a single cause and that causes can vary among people. Negative life events such as trauma, bereavement, unemployment, or significant life changes can increase the risk of Depression.

Having a medical condition such as cancer, stroke, or chronic pain can increase the risk. Using alcohol or drugs can increase the risk, either directly or as a result of withdrawal. Having unrealistic rules that govern how you think and behave, such as "I should be better by now" or "I must not let my family see that I'm upset", can increase the risk. (Beck, and Alford, 2009)

There's no single cause of Depression. It can occur for various reasons, and it has many different triggers. For some people, an upsetting or stressful life event, such as bereavement, divorce, illness, redundancy, and job or money worries, can be the cause. Different causes can often combine to trigger Depression. Research suggests that **genetic, biological, environmental, and psychological factors** play a role in Depression. Risk factors for Depression can include a personal or family history of Depression, significant negative life changes, trauma, or stress.

Clinical Depression, also known as major depressive disorder, is a severe mental disorder that can affect how a **person feels, thinks, and functions in their daily life.** It's characterized by a **persistent** low mood, low self-esteem, and a loss of interest in usually enjoyable activities. Signs and symptoms of clinical Depression may include Feelings of sadness, tearfulness, emptiness or hopelessness. Angry outbursts, irritability or frustration, even over small matters. Loss of interest or pleasure in most or all normal activities, such as sex, hobbies or sports. (Hammen, 2005)

Spiritual Root Cause Of Depression

Spiritual Depression is a term that people may use to describe feelings of disconnection from their religion or spirituality or a lack of a higher power in their life. It can also refer to a general feeling of sadness or melancholy. Spiritual Depression can have many causes. Everyday stressors and trials can contribute to spiritual distress. Not having enough time for religious activities, such as prayer, Bible study, or worship, can lead to spiritual Depression.

Deep questioning about the meaning of life, existence, and one's role in the universe can lead to existential angst and spiritual distress. A major loss in your life, such as a loss in your family or friend circle, a job loss, or a loss of God's spirit, can cause Depression. You may feel depressed and frustrated if you feel that your lifestyle is meaningless, but you've **been repressing your spiritual self. (Blazer, D2011)**

Spiritual Depression doesn't always stem from a religious belief or background. It can also stem from having a strong connection to things outside ourselves, such as nature or the universe. Depression results from a loss on a spiritual level. Existential questions: Unanswered existential questions can lead to spiritual Depression. Spiritual community issues: Struggles within a religious or spiritual community, such as judgment, exclusion, or conflicts with others, can contribute to a sense of isolation. (Blazer, D2011)

Religious trauma, also known as religious trauma syndrome (RTS), is a term used to describe the negative mental health effects of harmful or unhealthy religious experiences. It can include any traumatic experience that occurs in a religious or spiritual setting, Being forced to give money or resources or to be intimate or have sex against your will and being pressured to stay in an unhealthy relationship by using faith against you or being shamed for expressing your identity and being instilled with a fear of damnation or punishment from divine sources, or growing up with chronic fear of hell, Satan, demons, or salvation and being forced to be intimate with someone in a religious setting. Some common symptoms of religious trauma include Feeling shame about your identity, sexuality, or body; Having physical reactions to sexual thoughts, such as crying or feeling disconnected from your body; Having triggers that cause intense anxiety, panic, or shutting down; Feeling like you can't trust yourself, your body, or your emotions. (Downie, 2022).

Treatment.

Education, lifestyle changes, social support and psychological therapy are essential treatments for Depression. People may also require antidepressant medication. Medications may take up to six weeks to be effective, so be patient. Take the time to find the treatment that's right for you. Medications and psychotherapy are effective for most people with Depression. Your primary care doctor or psychiatrist can prescribe medications to relieve symptoms. However, many people with Depression also benefit from seeing a psychiatrist, psychologist or other mental health professional.

Transpersonal Approach to Dealing with Depression

Transpersonal therapy is a holistic approach to counselling that can be used to treat Depression and other mood and behavioural disorders. It's based on the idea that a healthy spirit plays a role in healing and integrates spiritual traditions and rituals into modern psychology. Transpersonal therapy can help people open to exploring their spirituality or having trouble finding meaning in their lives. Transpersonal therapy aims to increase one's sense of self and improve one's overall quality of life via spirituality and self-understanding. It's a therapy often used to address conditions with challenges related to self-worth and life purpose, such as anxiety and Depression. Transpersonal therapists use meditation, guided visualization, hypnotherapy, dream work, art, music, journaling, and mindfulness practices to help clients explore their spiritual selves and create meaning.

Biblical Psychology Approach to Dealing with Depression

He lifted me out of the pit of **despair,** the mud and the mire. Psalm 40: 1-2. The spirit of heaviness can be characterized as any intense negative feeling that challenges our faith and what we know about God. Heaviness may result from habitual sins like addiction, lying, gossip, or losing a job or even a loved one. Translations call it "despair, broken hearts, sorrow or discouragement. It can also mean feeble or weak. A person feeling the influence of the **spirit of heaviness** may feel like the things they used to do with ease now look overwhelming. Heaviness always has the **sense of anxiety, sorrow, grief,** etc. de'aghah, "fear," "dread," "anxious care" (Proverbs 12:25, "Heaviness in the heart of a man maketh it stoop," the Revised Version margin "or care"); kehah, "to be feeble," "weak" (Isaiah 61:3, "the spirit of heaviness"); panim, "face," "aspect" Job 9:27. (Devika, 2019)

When a lot happens in your life or the world around you, all the different thoughts, feelings and emotions you experience can build up and leave your energy heavy and dense. Over time, as these energies accumulate, they can affect how you feel and live. **Chronic Depression is** a type of Depression that lasts for a long time. Persistent depressive disorder (PDD), also known as dysthymia, is a chronic depression that's milder than major depressive disorder but can still be ongoing. PDD is characterized by a depressed mood that lasts for **at least two years,** along with other symptoms that are present for most of the day, on most days, for that same period of time. Symptoms can't be absent for more than two months in a row to meet the criteria for PDD.

Transpersonal Cognitive Behavioural Therapy sees chronic Depression as a spirit, not an emotion, and can be considered a **spiritual stronghold.** Depression can be caused by disappointments, unfulfilled expectations, or **generational curses,** and it can make it challenging to find a way out. Chronic Depression can be overcome by casting out the spirit of Depression and fear, and that perfect love can cast out all fear and torment.

Research links rumination, or repetitive dark, hopeless, or negative thoughts, to Depression. It follows, then, that overfocusing on spiritual fears or worries, mainly when you can't come up with any clear answers, can intensify spiritual Depression. Harmful **thought patterns** or messages from the **spiritual outside world** have left a lasting impression on the minds and hearts of people suffering from chronic Depression. Over time, these beliefs can become strongholds in the spiritual realm that people need to destroy using the truth of God's Word plus the Anointing of The Holy Spirit. (Lowery, 2022).

Spiritual Vision-The Cure For Hopelessness of Depression.

There is an old saying: "**A person without a vision is a person without a future. A person without a future will always return to the past.**" And Helen Keller wrote: The only thing worse than being blind is having sight with no vision. Proverbs 29:18 says, "Where there is no vision, the people are unrestrained." **They can't focus, can't reach their goal, can't follow their dream.** An older translation says, "**Without vision, the people perish.**" Without Vision, people lose the vitality that makes them feel alive. "**When there is no vision, there is no hope**" suggests that without clear goals or aspirations, it becomes difficult to feel optimistic or motivated. It implies that having a sense of purpose or direction is crucial for maintaining a positive outlook on life. Vision produces discipline.

When you see a strong vision, you will see disciplined people. Where there is no vision, there is no discipline. Hopelessness means no hope, the feeling that hopes have been destroyed or of facing a dilemma that cannot be solved. It is a subjective emotion that has a negative viewpoint for the future- one of losing control, confidence, courage, and the energy to reach one's goal. Medication can bring hope. Just talking to a therapist cannot inspire hope for your future. Divinely inspired Vision for the future births hope. (Barna, 2009).

Reference

- Beck, A.T. and Alford, B.A., 2009. Depression: Causes and treatment. University of Pennsylvania Press.
- Hammen, C., 2005. Stress and Depression. Annu. Rev. Clin. Psychol., 1(1), pp.293-319.
- Blazer, D.G., 2011. Spirituality and Depression. Religious and Spiritual Issues in Psychiatric Diagnosis. Arlington, VA: American Psychiatric Publishing, Inc, pp.1-22.
- Downie, A., 2022. Christian shame and religious trauma. Religions, 13(10), p.925.
- Devika, U., 2019. Lighthearted: Breaking Free from Heaviness. Balboa Press.

- Lowery, E.W., 2022. Destroying the Yoke of Bondage. Page Publishing Inc.
- Barna, G., 2009. The Power of Vision: Discover and Apply God's Vision for Your Life & Ministry. Gospel Light Publications.

Chapter 9- Transpersonal Approach To Dealing With Schizophrenia.

Schizophrenia usually involves delusions (false beliefs), hallucinations (seeing or hearing things that don't exist to outside observers), unusual physical behaviour, and disorganized thinking and speech. It is common for people with schizophrenia to have paranoid thoughts or hear voices. When schizophrenia is active, symptoms can include delusions, hallucinations, disorganized speech, trouble with thinking and lack of motivation. Cognitive symptoms include problems in attention, concentration, and memory. These symptoms can make it hard to follow a conversation, learn new things, or remember appointments. A person's level of cognitive functioning is one of the best predictors of their day-to-day functioning. (Van Os, Kenis, and Rutten, 2010).

Treatment

Lifelong treatment with medicines and psychosocial therapy can help manage schizophrenia, **though there is no cure for it, according to conventional psychology.** These treatments are needed even when symptoms ease. Some people may need to stay in a hospital during a crisis if symptoms are severe. Schizophrenia is usually treated with a combination of medication and therapy that's tailored to the individual. The goal of treatment is to help people manage schizophrenia and reduce the impact it has on their lives, even **though there's no cure.** Treatment is often lifelong and may need to continue even when symptoms improve. Medication Antipsychotics are often the first medication used to treat schizophrenia. They work by blocking how the brain uses certain chemicals for cell-to-cell communication. Other drugs may also be prescribed to treat symptoms that occur alongside schizophrenia or to reduce the side effects of antipsychotics.

Psychosocial therapy can help people develop recovery skills, such as setting and achieving goals. Cognitive behavioural therapy (CBT): A talk therapy method that can help people cope with and manage their condition. Psychoeducation: Helps people learn about schizophrenia. Family therapy and support: Helps people get support from their family. Medication and therapy can help manage the symptoms of schizophrenia. In many cases, people with schizophrenia can pursue their goals, have healthy relationships, keep jobs, and be productive members of their communities. (McCutcheon, Marques, and Howes, 2020)

Limitations Of Medical Model Psychotherapy.

The medical model may not accurately describe what happens in psychotherapy. It may also obscure the fact that psychotherapy is an interpersonal process and that many clients use it for support and personal growth rather than treatment. Mental illness: The medical model may focus too much on biological factors and neglect other important factors like social and psychological factors. This can lead to incomplete explanations of illness, which may mean treatments aren't entirely effective.

The biomedical model may not consider how factors other than physical ones, like environment and psychosocial factors, impact health. Another limitation of the medical model is that it tends to pathologize ordinary human experiences and behaviours, such as sadness or anxiety. This can lead to over-diagnosis and over-treatment of mental health issues, which can have negative consequences for individuals who may be unnecessarily labelled as mentally ill. The medical model is criticized for seeing the impairment as the most critical part of the person and suggesting the person is helpless to do anything about this. The medical model is said to be deterministic as it indicates a particular problem will always mean a person cannot be equal. (Klerman, 1977).

Biopsychosocial Spiritual Model Psychotherapy.

The biopsychosocial-spiritual model is a holistic approach to patient care that considers the interaction between four aspects of a **person: biological, psychological, social, and spiritual.** The model is based on the idea that these aspects are distinct dimensions of a person and that each can be affected by a person's history and illness and interact with and affect other aspects. The model also acknowledges that illness can disrupt a person's biological relationships, affecting all other relational aspects of their life.

The model also recognizes that **spiritual well-being** can significantly impact mental health and overall quality of life and that "spiritual" can refer to many different aspects, from non-religious to deeply religious experiences. A biopsychosocial-spiritual model is a holistic approach that acknowledges the interaction between physical, psychological, social, and spiritual aspects of patient care and well-being (Beng, 2004).

A Spirit-centered approach to counselling emphasizes a set of assumptions that postulate that the **Spirit is always at work in the world,** most notably bringing healing and restoration to all of creation. These assumptions lead to practices that inform the entirety of the counselling endeavour. Transpersonal Mental health care practice is a Spirit-centered approach to mental health. Historically, mental illnesses like schizophrenia were often attributed to supernatural forces and spiritual beliefs. Some believed that schizophrenia was caused by **evil spirits, demon possession,** or divine retribution for perceived misdeeds. Religion and spirituality often play an essential part in many people's experiences of schizophrenia. For some sufferers, religious delusions or intense religiously based irrational thinking may be a component of their symptoms; for instance, they may believe that God has sent them to become a great prophet. (Saad, Medeiros, and Mosini, 2017).

A typical report from those with schizophrenia is some religious beliefs that many **medical practitioners consider to be delusional** — such as the belief that demons possess them, that a god is talking to them, that they are divine beings, or that they are prophets. The **demonological Theory** suggests that demons or supernatural forces play a role in influencing human behaviour and causing nefarious activities. This Theory can be seen in various contexts. People have struggled with the problem of evil since the beginning of time. **Where did evil come from?** That's the perennial question. But the question assumes that evil is real and must have a cause. (Krause, 2015)

The Reality of Demons is a clear testimony of the existence of the Devil and his demons on earth and their manifold operations in the affairs and lives of people. What are demons in the Bible? **They are fallen angels who serve the Devil in alluring people to destructive behaviours, false teaching, and separation from God.** When the unclean Spirit goes out of a man, it passes through waterless places seeking rest, and not finding any, it says, "I will return to my house from which I came." Then, it takes along seven other spirits that are more evil than itself (Luke 11:24, 26). Demons can exist outside or inside humans.

They can travel. They can communicate. Each one has a separate identity. They can remember things and make plans. They can evaluate and make decisions. They can combine forces. 2 Corinthians 4:4 **says**

Satan is "the god of this world." He subtly influences everyone in it (Ephesians 2:2), which has been the case throughout history. Satan's time as God of this world is almost over. After a "war in heaven" (verse 7), which Satan lost, "the great dragon was cast out, that old serpent, called the Devil, and Satan, which deceiveth the whole world: he was cast out into the earth, and his angels were cast out with him." Revelation 12:12 describes a time when Satan "knoweth that he hath but a short time."

The Theory of the devils is a theory of history: political and social crises arise from the deliberate actions of evil or misguided leaders rather than as a natural result of conditions. People with schizophrenia may experience religious delusions, including the belief that demons or spirits possess them. These delusions are a subcategory of religious delusions in psychosis and involve a distorted perception that demons or spirits are controlling their actions or mental processes.

Other religious beliefs that people with schizophrenia may have include: A god is talking to them, They are divine beings, and They are prophets. However, the spiritual reality of demonic spirits confirms that demons can communicate with People with schizophrenia. In addition, it is wrong for anyone to deny the reality existence of the voices speaking to them. The human sense of a spiritual reality is present in all known cultures. (Kelly, 2004).

Biblical Psychology - Answers for Schizophrenia

Jesus assured his followers: "I have given you authority to tread on serpents and scorpions, and over all the power of the enemy, and nothing shall hurt you" (Luke 10:19). To the followers of Christ, Satan and his demonic agents are but defeated enemies. The weapons we fight with are not the weapons of the world. On the contrary, they have the **divine power to demolish strongholds.** We demolish arguments and every pretension that sets itself up against the knowledge of God, and we take captive every thought to make it obedient to Christ. "'In the last days, God says, I will pour out my Spirit on all people. Your sons and daughters will prophesy, your young men will see visions, and your old men will dream dreams. (Acts 2:17 NIV).

God The Father, through Jesus Christ, is releasing us from bondage, the power of sin, and addictions. The power of the Holy Spirit is giving each of us new guidance and direction. Jesus said that when "**the Spirit of truth has come, He will guide you into all truth"** (John 16:13). (Kelly, 2004)

Reference.

- McCutcheon, R.A., Marques, T.R. and Howes, O.D., 2020. Schizophrenia—an overview. JAMA psychiatry, 77(2), pp.201-210.

- Van Os, J., Kenis, G. and Rutten, B.P., 2010. The environment and schizophrenia. Nature, 468(7321), pp.203-212.
- Klerman, G.L., 1977. Mental illness, the medical model, and psychiatry. The Journal of Medicine and Philosophy, 2(3), pp.220-243.
- Saad, M., De Medeiros, R. and Mosini, A.C., 2017. Are we ready for a true biopsychosocial–spiritual model? The many meanings of "spiritual". Medicines, 4(4), p.79.
- Krause, V., 2015. Witchcraft, demonology, and confession in early modern France. Cambridge University Press.
- Kelly, H.A., 2004. The Devil, Demonology, and Witchcraft: Christian Beliefs in Evil Spirits. Wipf and Stock Publishers.

Chapter 10- Transpersonal Approach to Dealing with Suicide Thoughts Patterns.

The act or an instance of ending one's own life voluntarily and intentionally is known as suicide. One that carries out or attempts to carry out the act of suicide. Suicide refers to when a person purposely ends their own life. Sometimes, people use the term "commit suicide" to describe this. People who are suicidal want to kill themselves or are in a mental state in which they will likely try to do so. Desire for one's death or the death of another. In Psychiatry, a suicidal desire, manifested by passivity, withdrawal, and absorption in nihilistic thoughts, may eventually lead to suicidal behaviour. (Harwitz, and Ravizza, 2000).

Every year 703, 000 people take their own lives, and many more people attempt suicide. Every suicide is a tragedy that affects families, communities and entire countries and has long-lasting effects on the people left behind. Suicide occurs throughout the lifespan and was the fourth leading cause of death among 15–29-year-olds globally in 2019. Suicide does not just happen in high-income countries but is a **global phenomenon in all regions of the world.** In fact, over 77% of global suicides occurred in low- and middle-income countries in 2019. While the link between suicide and mental disorders (in particular, depression and alcohol use disorders) and a previous suicide attempt is well established in high-income countries, many suicides happen impulsively in moments of crisis with a breakdown in the ability to deal with life stresses, such as financial problems, relationship break-up or chronic pain and illness. (https://www.who.int/news-room/fact-sheets/detail/suicide). Suicidal feelings can affect anyone of any age, gender or background at any time. (Jeon, 2011)

Treatment

Mental illness is a significant risk factor for suicide, though the relationship between the two is complex. People with mental illness do have a higher risk of suicide than the general population, but mental illness alone does not cause suicidal behaviour. Instead, it is more likely to be due to an interaction between their mental illness and adverse life events that may trigger suicidal thoughts. The risk of suicide is higher in people with multiple mental illnesses or those who have recently been discharged from psychiatric care. Because of these considerations, people experiencing a mental illness must receive appropriate treatment and care. Professional intervention and therapy for suicidal thoughts can help relieve symptoms of stress, depression, and other issues that cause a person to think about ending their own life.

Cognitive Behavioral Therapy (CBT) for suicidal ideation is effective because it helps individuals challenge negative worldviews and unhelpful or harmful thought patterns and understand how their thoughts relate to their feelings and actions. CBT is highly effective in treating people who have suicidal thoughts, and it often works relatively quickly, with people seeing results in as few as ten sessions in some cases. (Jeon, 2011)

Spirit is the cause of feelings like love, forgiveness, cleanliness, mercy, intelligence and truthfulness. Spirit is eternal. Spiritual thoughts are thoughts that originate from keeping in mind that we are spirits. They are thoughts which give us a conscience. They help us differentiate right from wrong.

A spiritual mindset is not just about having a set of uplifting beliefs. Instead, it refers to spiritually aligned beliefs that influence your reactions and behaviour. Your mindset is a frame of mind that helps you move towards outcomes. Suicide thought patterns have their origin in the spiritual realm. According to spiritualism, the spirit world is the world or realm inhabited **by both good and evil spirits** of various spiritual manifestations. This spirit world is regarded as an external environment for spirits. (Hick, 2013).

Purpose Spirituality is one of the protective factors against suicide. However, the spiritual needs of people with suicidal ideation have not yet been adequately identified. Spiritual well-being is the ability to establish meaning and find purpose through the connection to God, the divine Creator, and a sense of connection beyond the self. It can benefit our overall well-being by cultivating our sense of inner understanding and place in life.

A spiritual purpose is establishing a set of values, principles and beliefs that give life meaning to you and then using them to guide your decisions and actions. To find spiritual purpose, Pose a significant spiritual question that you'd like to explore or be more knowledgeable about Who is this God I believe in? How do I make sense of evil in the world and live with that? What is prayer? Respond by reflecting, meditating, or writing in your journal, and answer it through your life story. (Tirri and Quinn, 2010).

The spiritual dimension of life opens us to look and see beyond the surface of day-to-day events and discover something of depth, fullness, and richness. To be a spiritual person is to recognize that this moment is an opportunity to experience fulfilment and contentment in life. **God is a God of Purpose:** He Created all things for His Will to Fulfill His Purpose. All things were created – the entire universe was created because of God's will; God's will is the source. We have received an inheritance from God, for he chose us in advance and made everything work according to his plan. Therefore, every human has received an inheritance from the Divine Creator. This inheritance is not brought about by our will or desire but by God's will and for God's purposes. We are predestined to receive this inheritance.

Biblical Psychology Of Divine Purpose

Ephesians 1:11 explains predestination's purpose by telling us that predestination is "according to the purpose of him who works all things according to the counsel of his will." The counsel of God's will concerns

God's wisdom, plan, and thought processes. The word "counsel" suggests intelligence and an intelligent reason for acting, and God never wills apart from His counsel. "Before I formed you in the womb, I knew you" is a quote from the Bible, Jeremiah 1:5, in which God speaks to Jeremiah: Before I formed you in the womb, I knew you. Before you were born, I set you apart.

I appointed you as a prophet to the nations." Jeremiah 1:5 states that before Jeremiah was born, even before he was formed in his mother's womb, the Lord had specific plans for his life. Scholars widely interpret this passage to mean that God predestined the course of Jeremiah's life. You created my inmost being; you knit me together in my mother's womb. I praise you because I am fearfully and wonderfully made; your works are wonderful. I know that full well. God tells Jeremiah, "Before I formed you in the womb, I knew you." This means I've known you before, and there was you to be known by anyone else. Before you were in the womb, I knew you before I even began to form you there. I knew you, who you are, what you would do. Every human is a product of Divine Purpose. Your existence is not an experiment but a product of purpose from the intelligent Creator. (Andersen, 1983).

God is omniscient; He knows everyone before their conception and birth. God formed them in their mother's womb and had plans for them before their birth. The same is true of every person today. Every infant in the womb has inherent value as a unique creation of God and should be regarded as a person with a future. God created humans to "be fruitful and multiply" [Genesis 1:28]. Creating and carrying new life in your body reflects God's nature as Creator. Conceiving and giving birth to a child is a beautiful example of how God has uniquely designed women and their role in procreation. "For you formed my inward parts; you knitted me together in my mother's womb. I praise you, for I am fearfully and wonderfully made.

Wonderful are your works; my soul knows it very well. My frame was not hidden from you when I was being made in secret, intricately woven in the depths of the earth. (Psalm 139:13-16). Research indicates that having a purpose in life is good for mental health. For example, having a greater purpose in life was significantly associated with lower levels of depression and anxiety. (Murphy, 2009).

Divine Vision: The Cure For Suicide Ideation.

Psychological researchers define purpose as a goal-oriented source of meaning from a desire to make a difference in the world beyond oneself. The literature also suggests that purpose is a stable intention to accomplish something personally meaningful and productive. Social support and culture may influence the development of purpose in life.

To identify your purpose and vision, consider what you want to achieve and what is important to you. Once you have identified these things, you can write them down and put them into action. A sense of purpose in life is an underlying concept in positive psychology relating to overall well-being. Psychological researchers argue that a purpose in life refers only to those sources of meaning that are both goal-oriented and motivated by a desire to make a difference in the world beyond the self (Bronk & Dubon, 2016).

A vision in life is an image of the future that can help people understand what they want, who they want to be, and what they aspire to in life. A vision can also help people answer the **question "why"** in life. The dictionary defines vision as an act or power of anticipating what will or may come to be. Vision gives direction and a glimpse over our lives to make our goals and purpose become a reality.

To understand where we want ourselves to be, we must have a clear vision of our life. Where there is no vision, the people perish. – Where there is **no prophetic vision or revelation from God,** the people cast off restraint and engage in destructive behaviour. There is an old saying: "A person without a vision is a person without a future. A person without a future will always return to the past." And Helen Keller wrote: The only thing worse than being blind is having sight with no vision. **"When there is no vision, there is no hope"** suggests that without clear goals or aspirations, it becomes difficult to feel optimistic or motivated. It implies that having a sense of purpose or direction is crucial for maintaining a positive outlook on life.

Reference

- Harwitz, D. and Ravizza, L., 2000. Suicide and depression. Emergency Medicine Clinics of North America, 18(2), pp.263-271.

- Jeon, H.J., 2011. Depression and suicide. Journal of the Korean Medical Association, 54(4), pp.370-375.
- Hick, J., 2013. The fifth dimension: An exploration of the spiritual realm. Simon and Schuster.
- Tirri, K. and Quinn, B., 2010. Exploring the role of religion and spirituality in the development of purpose: Case studies of purposeful youth. British Journal of Religious Education, 32(3), pp.201-214.
- Murphy, G.L., 2009. Divine action and divine purpose. Currents in Theology and Mission, 36(1), pp.32-39.
- Andersen, W.E., 1983. A biblical view of education. Journal of Christian Education, (2), pp.15-30.
- Bronk, K.C., Purpose Through the Lens of Character Virtue Development. In The Routledge International Handbook of Multidisciplinary Perspectives on Character Development, Volume I (pp. 611-629). Routledge.

Chapter 11- Transpersonal Psychodynamic Theory.

Freud believed human behaviour could be explained by **intrapsychic processes** and interpersonal patterns outside of a person's conscious awareness and based on **childhood experiences.** A general definition of psychodynamic theory is that forces outside of a person's awareness explain why they behave a certain way. Psychodynamic theory (sometimes called psychoanalytic theory) explains personality through unconscious psychological processes (for example, wishes and fears of which we're not fully aware) and contends that childhood experiences are crucial in shaping adult personality.

Freud's psychoanalytic theory, which emphasizes the **unconscious mind,** has fundamentally altered our perception of human behaviour. He proposed that our **conscious thoughts** do not always govern our actions but are often driven by unconscious desires and experiences. (Guntrip, 2018)

Psychodynamic therapy relies on the interpersonal interactions between the therapist and client to reveal the content of the person's unconscious, including their deepest fears and wishes, along with defences that guard inner conflicts from the person's awareness. The goal of psychoanalysis was to study the **unconscious mind.** To Freud, understanding the unconscious mind was crucial in determining an individual's motivations and behaviours.

Psychoanalysis therapy aims to release **repressed** emotions and experiences, i.e. make the unconscious conscious. Psychoanalysis is commonly used to treat depression and anxiety disorders. Only by having a cathartic (**healing)** experience can a person be **helped and "cured". (Summers, Barber, and Zilcha-Mano, 2024)**

The unconscious mind is a psychological concept that refers to the part of the mind that is not readily available for introspection but is thought to influence conscious thought and behaviour. It includes thoughts, memories, urges, and feelings we don't know we are having or have "**repressed" (hidden from ourselves).** The unconscious mind is often described using the metaphor of an iceberg, with the conscious mind being the visible tip, the preconscious just below the surface, and the unconscious being the submerged portion. The unconscious mind is thought to contain unacceptable or unpleasant contents, such as feelings of pain, anxiety, or conflict. It also allows contradictory ideas to coexist, and its contents are not arranged chronologically.

The unconscious mind is a reservoir of feelings, thoughts, urges, and memories outside our conscious awareness. You have no immediate access to what resides in your subconscious, but **it controls 95% of how you think, react, and behave,** your actions, and how you perceive life. Examples of unconscious events include **suppressed feelings, auto reactions,**

complexes, and concealed phobias. Historically, emotions, thoughts, and responses outside of a human's consciousness were attributed to a divine's role in dictating a motive or action. It can be accessed through various techniques, such as **meditation, hypnosis, and visualization**. By unlocking the power of the subconscious mind, we can become more aware of our thoughts, feelings, and behaviours, which can help us make better choices and achieve our goals. (Bargh, and Morsella, 2008)

The Unconscious Mind

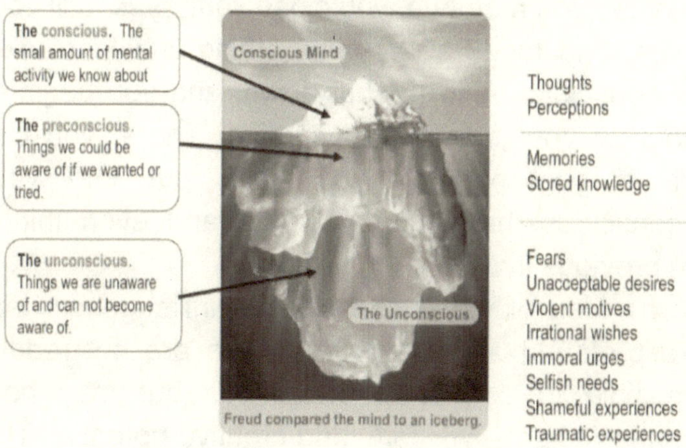

Freud compared the mind to an iceberg.

The idea of the **unconscious spirit**, or **spiritual unconscious,** is a concept that has been explored in many spiritual and philosophical traditions throughout history. It suggests that deeper aspects of ourselves are not easily accessible to conscious awareness but may contain important insights, wisdom, and creative potential. In some religious traditions, the unconscious spirit may be seen as the **source of divine inspiration** or guidance.

Viktor Frankl described the spiritual unconscious as a higher aspect of the self, a personal attribute, and a "transpersonal" and "transhuman" agent. The subconscious mind is also considered to be a direct link to **universal consciousness,** which is the **source of all power and creativity.** It is the source of insight, intuition, imagination, and creativity. Learning to read and understand the unconscious mind is a basic tenet of mindful meditation and coaching, and it can improve lives.

When you meditate, you close your eyes, still your senses, and focus on your breathing, which causes your conscious mind to shut down, and you begin to encounter your subconscious mind. There, you can start to see patterns you have put into your subconscious throughout your life and even things from previous lives.

The idea of the unconscious spirit suggests that more profound aspects of ourselves are not readily accessible to conscious awareness but may hold essential insights, wisdom, and creative potential. The Higher Self is the Wise Being within you. The higher self is associated with multiple belief systems, but its basic premise describes an eternal, omniscient, conscious, and intelligent being who is one's authentic self. The higher self, also known as the supraconscious or superconscious mind, is a dimension that exists beyond the conscious and subconscious mind.

It's associated with multiple belief systems and is often described as a **spiritual or transcendent aspect of consciousness.** The higher self is said to transcend individual experiences and connect with higher states of consciousness and universal wisdom. It's also referred to as an eternal, omniscient, conscious, and intelligent being that is one's real self.

On the other hand, the subconscious mind is often referred to as the lower self or inner child. It's involved in information processing, affects everything we think, say, and do, and stores our beliefs and values. It also determines our memories and monitors the information around us, deciding what to send to the conscious mind and what to store for later.

Exploring and aligning the higher self and the subconscious mind can lead to a deeper understanding of one's purpose and authentic self. Your higher self is a powerful extension of yourself. The most enlightened version of you, free from ego and aligned with the universe's most profound truths. The higher self embodies wisdom, peace, and an understanding transcending everyday consciousness. (de Carvalho, and Moreira-Almeida, 2024).

Transpersonal development is the idea that there are developmental stages that go beyond the adult ego and that these stages involve experiences of connectedness with phenomena that are outside the ego's boundaries. The term "transpersonal" literally means "beyond the personal." Spiritual development is exploring **one's spiritual identity** and connection to something greater than oneself. It can involve developing an **awareness of realities beyond time and space** and believing in something beyond the material universe. It can also include searching for meaning and purpose and developing personal values. Spiritual development can take place within or outside of a religious framework.

It's not the same as having a particular faith; a person can be spiritual without a religion. Spiritual development relates to fundamental questions about the meaning and purpose of life, which affect everyone and is not dependent on **religious affiliation.** Spiritual development is not about becoming more spiritual. It is about realizing or becoming **more and more aware of one's natural, innate spirituality. (Assagioli, 1991)**

Spiritual Development and Transpersonal Psychodynamic Theory.

Spiritual development, in essence, is to believe in something beyond the material universe and to develop an awareness of realities beyond the confines of time and space. This belief originates from a connection of your spirit to God the Creator. A creator deity or God is responsible for creating the world, universe, and Earth. In monotheism, the single God is often also the Creator. Creation is the basis of God's presence throughout the universe and a universal revelation of **his lordship.** It is also believed to motivate worship.

He is THE Creator because "Through him, all things were made; **without him, nothing was made that has been made"** (John 1:3). God's consciousness, or God's mind, is a concept that may refer to a state of consciousness that transcends ordinary human consciousness. It can also refer to a state of liberation from the limitations of the ego or self-concept or a **mystical experience** that transcends the perceived separation between the self and the world or God. God's consciousness is a mind free of fear, confusion, and delusion that naturally knows the path to one's true calling. Your spiritual development eliminates the negative influence of your unconscious mind on your personality. (Morris, 2022)

Transpersonal Mental Health Care practice focuses **on Healing** and integrating the splits and inner divisions that occur through social and cultural conditioning among the physical, emotional, mental, and spiritual aspects of a person's being (Vaughan, 1993). The healer channels energy from a divine or universal source to the patient to heal their mind, body, and spirit. The word "spiritual" comes from the Latin word spiritus, which means "breath of life."

Spiritual Healing can help with a variety of physical, mental, and emotional conditions, including depression and broken bones. A treatment involves the transfer of energy from the healer to the recipient. In Transpersonal Mental Health Care practice, **the healer is the Person Of The Holy -Spirit.** The gift of Healing is when the Holy Spirit supernaturally heals someone from a disease or infirmity. Feeling the Holy Spirit can be a physical sensation, as our bodies are designed to respond to God's presence. When the Holy Spirit enters a person's life, they may feel Warmth and embrace, Tingling and electricity. (Gaiser, 2010).

The spiritual aspect of Healing refers to **spiritual energy** working intensely on our spiritual being. Healing involves the transfer of energy; in other words, it is not from the transpersonal therapist, but the spiritual counsellor links with the Person Of The Holy Spirit's Universal' or Divine energy to channel healing **for the mind, body, and spirit.**

Reference

- Guntrip, H.Y., 2018. Personality structure and human interaction: The developing synthesis of psychodynamic theory. Routledge.
- Summers, R.F., Barber, J.P. and Zilcha-Mano, S., 2024. Psychodynamic Therapy. Guilford Publications.
- Bargh, J.A. and Morsella, E., 2008. The unconscious mind. Perspectives on psychological science, 3(1), pp.73-79.
- de Carvalho, J.M. and Moreira-Almeida, A., 2024. Existential meaning, spiritual unconscious and spirituality in Viktor Frankl. Journal of Religion and Health, 63(1), pp.31-45.
- Assagioli, R., 1991. Transpersonal development. Patrick Stephens.
- Morris, H., 2022. Biblical creationism. New Leaf Publishing Group.
- Gaiser, F.J., 2010. Healing in the Bible: Theological Insight for Christian ministry. Baker Academic.

Chapter 12- Transpersonal Approach to Dealing with Trauma.

Trauma is the lasting emotional response that often results from living through a distressing event. Experiencing a traumatic event can harm a person's sense of safety, sense of self, and ability to regulate emotions and navigate relationships. Trauma is a pervasive problem. It results from exposure to an incident or series of emotionally disturbing or life-threatening events with lasting adverse effects on the individual's functioning and mental, physical, social, emotional, and spiritual well-being.

Traumatic experiences often involve a threat to life or safety. Still, any situation that leaves you feeling overwhelmed and isolated can result in trauma, even if it doesn't involve physical harm. It's not the objective circumstances determining a traumatic event; it is your subjective emotional experience. Childhood trauma can result from anything that disrupts a child's sense of safety, including. (Van der Kolk, 2003)

Childhood traumatic stress occurs when violent or dangerous events overwhelm a child's or adolescent's ability to cope. Traumatic events may include Neglect and psychological, physical, or sexual abuse: natural disasters, terrorism, and community and school violence. All five forms of childhood trauma in a study (witnessing violence, physical Neglect, emotional abuse, physical abuse, and sexual abuse) demonstrated statistically significant relationships with the number of different aggressive behaviours reported in adulthood.

The effects of childhood trauma may seem like they can't be cured. But with the right approach, you can overcome childhood trauma and learn to cope. Studies show emotional abuse may be the most damaging form of maltreatment, causing adverse developmental consequences equivalent to, or more severe than, those of other forms of abuse. Unhealed **childhood wounds** can manifest themselves in a variety of ways, including feelings of fear, low self-esteem, insecurity, PTSD, and difficulty forming trusting relationships. (Krystal, 1978)

Repressed childhood trauma is a defence mechanism that occurs when a child's mind unconsciously blocks painful memories from conscious memory to protect them from psychological harm. This trauma can stem from many adverse experiences. Repressed childhood trauma is common among adults and may not be remembered until later in life. It can cause various emotional problems in adulthood, such as low self-esteem, feelings of shame and inadequacy, or poor boundaries.

People with repressed childhood trauma may also confabulate or fill in memory gaps with false information to unconsciously protect themselves from the pain of remembering. The result is feelings of shame and worthlessness that are developed in childhood. Experiences of childhood trauma such as abuse, Neglect, or witnessing violence can cause these feelings and often lead to several problems in adulthood, including depression, anxiety, and substance abuse. Childhood trauma can be buried in the subconscious mind in the subcortical regions of the brain, making it difficult to access consciously.

Psychotherapy modalities like trauma-focused cognitive behavioural therapy (TF-CBT) or cognitive processing therapy (CPT) can help people understand and manage their thoughts, feelings, and behaviours related to childhood trauma. (Cohen, 1985)

Adults with repressed childhood trauma often experience a wide range of intense emotions without apparent triggers. These emotional signs are not just fleeting moments of sadness or stress; they are deep-seated reactions stemming from traumatic events that were never processed. Repressed memories can often be recovered when someone encounters something that reminds them of a traumatic event, such as familiar sights, sounds, or scents. When this happens, it's typical for a person to feel emotionally flooded by the memory and the complex feelings associated with it.

Some psychologists believe that people who have experienced childhood trauma can develop large-scale difficulties with recalling early life events. This phenomenon is often called "dissociative amnesia" (or sometimes "traumatic dissociative amnesia"). Some survivors have unconsciously blocked out weeks, months, or even years of their childhoods. This is often the result of a child dissociating from a traumatic experience. Dissociation involves detaching from your thoughts, feelings, or even your body and is a frequent occurrence in trauma survivors. (Goodman, Gonzalves, and Wolpe, 2019).

Given that trauma frequently leads to a need to find meaning and that spirituality often provides such a meaning system in people's lives, it follows that trauma can introduce a need to reconcile complex events with beliefs. Trauma affects everyone differently, and some people may not even realize when they're carrying trauma from childhood, an experience sometimes referred to as subconscious trauma or unresolved childhood trauma. Healing from childhood trauma can involve a variety of techniques, including therapy, support, and stress reduction. Spending time with friends, family, or support groups can help people feel less isolated and connect with others in meaningful ways. People can also discuss their feelings with someone they trust, such as a counsellor.

Healing from childhood trauma involves addressing the emotional, mental, and physical **wounds** you've experienced. Working with a trauma-informed therapist is essential—they can help you accept what happened and grieve its impact. Seeking therapy, practising self-care, developing a support system, and considering medication are all effective ways to treat childhood trauma in adults. Religious practices such as prayer are exercises in religious reframing.

Meditation and mindfulness activities that can reduce arousal, acceptance and forgiveness activities that control negative emotions like anger, guilt and shame, as well as nurture empathy, have each been found to help individuals with childhood trauma. Spirituality can be helpful when a positive relationship to one's beliefs and practices buffers the effects of trauma and provides comfort during times of distress. (Carr and Hancock, 2017)

Biblical Psychology Approach To Trauma.

We can finally release our grief because we are being comforted in God's loving arms, in the arms of others who love us, and even in our compassionate arms. This grief comes with a promise of blessing and healing. "Blessed are those who mourn," Jesus said, "for they will be comforted" (Matthew 5:4). "The Lord is close to the brokenhearted and saves those **who are crushed in spirit"** (Ps 34:18). "My flesh and my heart may fail, but God is the strength of my heart and my portion forever" (Ps 73:26). **"He heals the brokenhearted and binds up their wounds" (Ps 147:3**). Through Jesus' wounds, we can be healed and gain eternal life. (Isaiah 53:5). The Comforter In the Gospel occurs in John 14:16,26; 15:26; 16:7 and refers to the Holy Spirit.

The word literally means "called to one's side" for help. But the Comforter (Counselor, Helper, Intercessor, Advocate, Strengthener, Standby), the Holy Spirit, Whom the Father will send in My name [in My place, to represent Me and act on My behalf], He will teach you all things. But I will send you the Comforter from the Father. When he comes, he will give evidence about me. He is the Spirit of truth who comes from the Father. So "comfort" literally means "with strength". So when the King James translators used the word "comforter" to refer to the Holy Spirit, they weren't telling us that the Holy Spirit would come to us to make our lives easy and pain-free. God sent Him to us to provide strength in our times of struggle.

In verse 16, Jesus introduces the role of the Holy Spirit as our Helper. You could say the Spirit is the big **'C' Counselor.** He provides assistance, support, relief, advocacy, and guidance. He is the great Paraclete who offers the things so many people desperate**ly seek in therapy. Isaiah 61:3 says that the Lord our Counselor can make us oaks of righteousness. (Baldwin, 2018)**

Reference

- Van der Kolk, B.A., 2003. Psychological trauma. American Psychiatric Pub.
- Krystal, H., 1978. Trauma and effects. The psychoanalytic study of the child, 33(1), pp.81-116.
- Cohen, J., 1985. Trauma and repression. Psychoanalytic Inquiry, 5(1), pp.163-189.
- Goodman, G.S., Gonzalves, L. and Wolpe, S., 2019. False memories and true memories of childhood trauma: Balancing the risks. Clinical Psychological Science, 7(1), pp.29-31.

- Carr, S.M. and Hancock, S., 2017. Healing the inner child through portrait therapy: Illness, identity and childhood trauma. International Journal of Art Therapy, 22(1), pp.8-21.
- Baldwin, J., 2018. Trauma-sensitive theology: Thinking theologically in the era of trauma. Wipf and Stock Publishers.

Chapter 13- Transpersonal Approach To Healing Of Emotional wounds.

An emotional wound is a negative experience that causes psychological pain and can last for weeks, months, or even years. Specific events, repeated trauma, or ongoing situations can cause emotional wounds. You are witnessing a murder, experiencing the death of a child, or being caught in an avalanche. Repeated trauma: Being bullied at work or having a **series of toxic relationships**. Ongoing situations: Growing up in a violent cult, living in poverty, or experiencing childhood neglect from addicted parents. Emotional wounds can impact our relationships, happiness, and overall well-being. Warning signs of emotional distress: Anger, feeling edgy or lashing out at others, Overwhelming sadness, Pulling away from people and things, Lacking Energy or constantly feeling tired, and Feeling like you have to keep busy. (Benner, 2016)

An "emotional wound" is a problematic, traumatizing or harmful experience (or set of experiences) that causes you **mental and psychological pain.** This pain goes on and on, lasting weeks, months or even years if the wound is deep enough. **Emotional damage** resulting from trauma can manifest in various ways. Individuals may experience symptoms such as intense fear, anxiety, depression, anger, guilt, shame, or a sense of emotional numbness. Psychological Concerns: Anxiety and panic attacks, fear, anger, irritability, obsessions and compulsions, shock and disbelief, emotional numbing and detachment, depression, shame and guilt are Emotional Trauma Symptoms. (Ricciardi, et al, 2013).

Identify the feeling that dominates and oppresses you. Underline the words that come up most often. If none can be summed up precisely in the five wounds (**rejection, abandonment, humiliation, betrayal and injustice**), pick out those closest to them or describe them differently. Not everyone returns to emotional health. Some people continue to experience deep emotional pain, repeat unhealthy behaviours and relationships, and struggle with negative, distorted thoughts. Emotional healing is possible.

Emotional healing involves seven stages: awareness, acceptance, processing, release, growth, integration, and transformation. Self-care can help you heal emotional pain. You can try learning mindfulness and grounding exercises, requesting support from friends, and labelling your emotions. For long-term emotional pain, you may want to consider seeking the help of a professional who can support you with therapy techniques and medications.

Emotional wounds and spiritual wounds can both disrupt a person's life. These can be caused by significant events, often in childhood, that lead to **suppressed pain** and emotions. These wounds can manifest as emotional overreactions, such as an overwhelming fear of losing people or a long-term fear of embarrassment. Humiliation can stem from being ridiculed or demeaned in public and affect self-respect and dignity. (Feinstein, 2023)

Abandonment: This can manifest as an overwhelming fear of losing people, leading to isolation and loneliness. Spiritual wounds can disrupt a person's relationship with God or their spiritual practices. They can occur when an authority figure, parent, or religious leader uses God's name for self-centred purposes or twists God's word to cause harm. Another example of a spiritual wound is when someone questions their belief in a higher being or entity after being involved in an incident—feelings of anger, confusion, and bitterness toward God: toxic shame, self-denial and self-hatred.

Unholy fear of God's wrath or punishment. Anxiety or disassociation when it comes to spiritual practices. A core wound is a deep emotional wound, often formed from suppressed pain and emotions internalized from a significant event, usually in childhood. This pain will likely grow and create a belief system about the self, often leading to compensating behaviours to manage the pain. (Aiken, 2022)

The messy reality of those **"wounds,"** which may result from traumatic events, grief, and heartbreak, is that they **can heal over time.** They might also heal quickly. Or not at all. How our brains deal with traumatic events may have more to do with the healing process than time. Spiritual wounding is, essentially, the violation of the sacred or **spiritual core in human**

beings, harm experienced at the deepest level of one's being.

Soul wounding is An overlooked, unassessed emotional, spiritual, or psychosocial wound that traumatically or insidiously Separates one from one's sense of self. Soul draining: Constant work, emotional and mental stress, tension, lack of sleep, and lack of proper exercise can lead to exhaustion. It is vital to trace the root of your tiredness: the people we surround ourselves with significantly impact the emotional Energy we carry

Emotional and spiritual Energy are two of the four dimensions of human Energy: physical and mental Energy. Some say that physical Energy is the most fundamental source, while spiritual Energy is the most significant. Here are some ways to access and manage these types of Energy. Emotional Energy is closely linked to feelings and can be expressed through the emotions we put into the world. To increase the quality of emotional Energy, some say to experience positive emotions like enjoyment, challenge, and opportunity instead of negative emotions like fear, danger, or threat. Some say spiritual Energy is best accessed by maintaining a daily practice that keeps the connection open.

This could include a spiritual or religious practice or mindfulness, which involves focusing on the present moment and engaging the creative and intuitive parts of the brain. In harmony with all four dimensions of Energy, developing each one equally is essential. For example, some say that boundaries can help with energy management. (Prophet, and Spadaro, 2000)

The 4 Dimensions of Energy: Physical, Emotional, Mental and Spiritual. If any of these dimensions is under-stressed or over-stressed, our performance suffers. Spiritual Energy is the Energy generated by the inner self, which religious people call the soul. The connection with the Spirit of God determines one's spiritual Energy level. Soul energy, Also known as spirit energy, is the most subtle type of Energy and is closely affiliated with your emotions. "It can be translated in many different ways, such as your mind, Spirit, consciousness, vitality, expression, soul, and Energy.

The spiritual aspect refers to spiritual Energy working **intensely on our spiritual being.** Healing involves the transfer of Energy to our soul and the accommodation of the mind. Divine energy channels healing for the mind, body, and Spirit.

Biblical Psychology Of Divine Energy.

Divine Spiritual Energy could refer to the Energy generated by the Holy Spirit in the inner self, which some religious people call the soul. It could also refer to spiritual representations, forms, or prototypes that some say are based on the Anointing from different beliefs in the power of the Holy Spirit. But you will receive power when the Holy Spirit comes upon you. (Acts 1:8). They would "receive" power, but it wasn't power for political dominance or military conflicts. It was the power of the Holy Spirit—God dwelling within them and transforming them. Acts 1:8 promises, "The Holy Spirit will come upon you and give you power."

When the Holy Spirit comes upon you, you will experience an explosion that will change your whole life and, through you, help to change the world. It's tremendous. "Then, after doing all those things, I will pour out my Spirit upon all people. Your sons and daughters will prophesy. Your old men will dream dreams, and your young men will see visions. (Joel 2:28). Every human being can access Divine Spiritual Energy to heal emotional wounds by receiving the Holy Spirit. (Bradshaw, 2006)

Reference

- Benner, D.G., 2016. Healing emotional wounds. Wipf and Stock Publishers.
- Ricciardi, E., Rota, G., Sani, L., Gentili, C., Gaglianese, A., Guazzelli, M. and Pietrini, P., 2013. How the brain heals emotional wounds: the functional neuroanatomy of forgiveness. Frontiers in human neuroscience, 7, p.48075.
- Feinstein, D., 2023. Using energy psychology to remediate emotional wounds rooted in childhood trauma: preliminary clinical guidelines. Frontiers in Psychology, 14, p.1277555.
- Aiken, S., 2022. Spiritual Wounds: Trauma, Testimony and the Irish Civil War. Merrion Press.
- Prophet, E.C. and Spadaro, P.R., 2000. Your Seven Energy Centers: A Holistic

Approach to Physical, Emotional and Spiritual Vitality. Summit University Press.

- Bradshaw, D., 2006. The divine energies in the New Testament. SAINT VLADIMIRS THEOLOGICAL QUARTERLY, 50(3), p.189.

www.ingramcontent.com/pod-product-compliance
Lightning Source LLC
LaVergne TN
LVHW090420210926
848480LV00002B/635

* 9 7 9 8 2 3 0 2 0 5 5 7 9 *